LOST C...
TREVOSE

The Shipwreck, *c.*1805, by J.M.W.Turner.

LOST OFF TREVOSE

THE SHIPWRECKS OF CORNWALL'S TREVOSE HEAD

BRIAN FRENCH

To the Watchkeepers of NCI Stepper Point

First published 2011

The History Press
The Mill, Brimscombe Port
Stroud, Gloucestershire, GL5 2QG
www.thehistorypress.co.uk

British Library Cataloguing in Publication Data.
A catalogue record for this book is available from the British Library.

ISBN 978 0 7524 5689 8

Typesetting and origination by The History Press
Printed in Great Britain
Manufacturing managed by Jellyfish Print Solutions Ltd

CONTENTS

ACKNOWLEDGEMENTS

I would like to acknowledge the help and advice received in producing this book from the following:

Derek Lindsey, NCI Stepper Point and former Station Manager
John Buckingham and George Barnes of the Padstow Museum
The Libraries at Bodmin and Truro
Kim Cooper and staff at the Cornish Studies Centre, Redruth
John Puddicombe of the HMS *Warwick* Association
Ness Towndrow for her spectacular cover photo
Moira Gill of St Merryn for her HMS *Warwick* input

I have acknowledged the sources of photographs in the text. Unacknowledged photographs, sketches and maps are the author's own work.

And, of course, to my editors, Amy Rigg and Emily Locke of The History Press.

TERMS OF REFERENCE

In order to give some reasonable boundaries to this account I have followed roughly the work of Noall & Farr (1964) and Larne (1995) and taken for my geographical parameters the area between latitude 50.30.00N and 50.51.00N and longitude 05.00W and 05.38W. On the coast this covers the shore from Park Head in the south, round Trevose Head to Harlyn Bay in the east. Even with these arbitrary boundaries there are many losses to record and in the maps I have tried to plot each vessel's last location as near to the given point as possible.

The narrative will be supported by detailed tables listing vessel, date lost, location, crew saved/lost, tonnage, cargo, captain and maps showing the last known position of all vessels. Photographs, sketches and diagrams will illustrate the text. Where a vessel was positioned outside this 'rectangle' I have included it where historical significance or interest demanded.

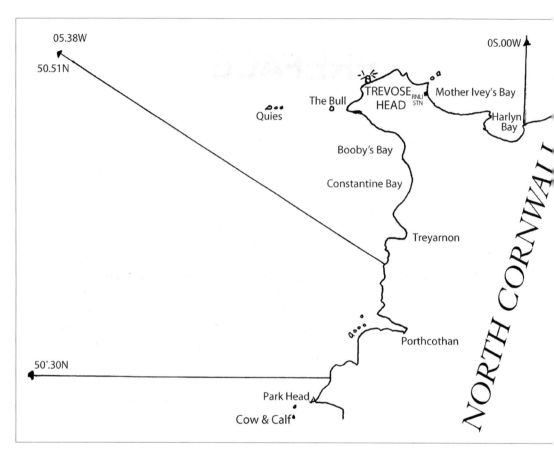

The scope of this book.

PREFACE

The book *Wrecks and Rescues around Padstow's Doom Bar* (2007) focussed predominantly on maritime activity within Padstow harbour limits. This second book now takes Trevose Head, the 'Lizard' of the north coast, as its focal point and tells the stories not only of those better-known ships wrecked on Trevose Head itself, but also those recorded as simply 'lost off Trevose'. This inhospitable coast has seen many disasters over the centuries, from ocean-going sailing ships blown off course or badly navigated, to coastal vessels bound for Wales and the Bristol Channel foundering, colliding, and 'colliers' blowing up. Both world wars saw intense activity off Trevose as German U-boats attempted to prevent supplies from reaching the UK and Europe. This book tells the story of these disparate events all linked by the location; Trevose Head.

In addition, the narrative attempts to come to terms with the question, 'Why did these disasters happen – at least the peacetime ones?' As a landsman, this author was initially baffled by the number of collisions occurring in these waters. Wasn't the sea big enough for everybody? This question leads us to the development of safety at sea, starting with the erection of Trevose lighthouse in 1857, a project strenuously opposed by most seafarers, and covering improvements in navigation (the discovery of longitude), International Sailing Law ('rules of the road') and the prevention of the overloading of cargo (Plimsoll Line).

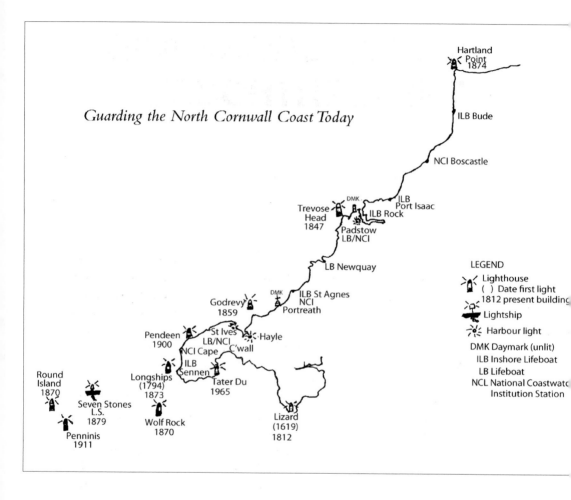

Guarding the North Cornwall Coast Today

Hartland Point 1874

ILB Bude

NCI Boscastle

DMK
Trevose Head 1847

ILB Port Isaac
ILB Rock
Padstow LB/NCI

LB Newquay

Godrevy 1859

DMK
ILB St Agnes
NCI Portreath

Pendeen 1900

St Ives LB/NCI
Hayle
NCI Cape
C'wall

ILB Sennen

Longships (1794) 1873

Tater Du 1965

Round Island 1870

Seven Stones L.S. 1879

Wolf Rock 1870

Lizard (1619) 1812

Penninis 1911

LEGEND
Lighthouse
( ) Date first light
1812 present building
Lightship
Harbour light
DMK Daymark (unlit)
ILB Inshore Lifeboat
LB Lifeboat
NCI National Coastwatch Institution Station

CHAPTER 1

THE IRON SHORE AND THE LIGHTHOUSE

The ship that will not obey the helm must obey the rocks.

Old Cornish Proverb

The north coast of Cornwall is famed today for its tourist potential with wide sandy beaches and excellent conditions for the relatively recent sport of surfing. Holidaymakers flock to the region throughout the year to take part in or watch this ever-growing pastime. This industry is flourishing on the pounding Atlantic waves which race into land unchecked after a journey of some 2,000 miles, these selfsame waves that in years before pounded ships to matchwood on Trevose's lee shore.

Ships on these waters are now monitored constantly by sophisticated radio, radar and computer systems operated by the Maritime and Coastguard Agency's regional headquarters at Falmouth, which is also the International Distress Centre. Immediate protection is afforded by the RNLI's latest and most powerful lifeboat, *Spirit of Padstow*, operating from its state-of-the-art boathouse on Trevose Head. The entire coast is signalled by a succession of lights and daymarks all the way from the Longships lighthouse off Land's End to Hartland Point light in the north. The newest recruit to sea safety is the National Coastwatch Institution, which has re-established visual watch stations in north Cornwall at Boscastle, Padstow, St Agnes and St Ives.

Yet even today the Nautical Almanac gives fairly bleak advice to the sailor:

The N coast of Cornwall and the SW approaches to the Bristol Channel are very exposed. Yachts need to be sturdy and well equipped since if bad weather develops, no shelter may be at hand … Bude dries and is not approachable in W winds… Boscastle is a tiny harbour (dries) … Padstow is a refuge but in strong NW winds the sea breaks on the Bar and prevents entry … Off Trevose Head beware the Quies Rocks… Newquay dries and is uncomfortable in N winds … off Godrevy Light are the Stones, a drying rocky shoal extending 1.5 m offshore … St Ives to Land's End is rugged and exposed…

From our relatively safe (and sane) vantage point of the twenty-first century it is astonishing to read that when in 1619 Sir John Killegrew of Arwenack, Governor of Pendennis Castle, petitioned the King that a lighthouse be built at the Lizard Point, Trinity House, the present controller of our lighthouses, opposed the erection, stating 'It is not necessary or convenient to erect a lighthouse there, but per contra, inconvenient having regard to pirates and enemies whom it would direct to a safe place of landing'. Killegrew himself added the telling comment: 'They (the locals) have been so long used to reap profit by the calamity of the ruin of shipping that they claim it (the wreck) as hereditary.'

There is no doubt that the mindset at the time was that well-built vessels would have no need of help or refuge as they could sail well off the coast and ride out any gales. In fact any move towards increasing the safety of vessels, both in those early days of sail and well into the nineteenth century, was looked on as unwarranted interference by Government in the ship owners' domain. It is perhaps a salient point that anyone can, even in today's safety-conscious society, put a boat onto water without any check on their competence or the suitability of the vessel. This freedom of operation has unfortunately led to inevitable tragedies in these waters.

Richard Larne goes further:

> What is remarkable and scarcely credible, is that no emphasis whatsoever was placed upon the need for a light at Land's End. At the very south-west 'toe' of England, ship's masters required sight of this headland, a landfall if possible, before continuing up the English or Bristol Channels or across the Atlantic or Bay of Biscay. Attempting to round Land's End at night carrying coal from North Wales must have been a nightmare.

The RNLI *Spirit of Padstow* at her dedication ceremony, July 2006.

Above: The new Padstow RNLI Station at Mother Ivey's Bay.

Left: Ever watchful at NCI Stepper Point, Padstow.

Killegrew did get his wish however, and was allowed to display a light at Land's End provided, as Trinity House decreed, 'that it should be extinguished at the approach of the enemy'. More consternation was to follow when James I allowed Killegrew, now running low on funds, to set a fee of one halfpenny per ton on all vessels passing his light. Uproar ensued, Killegrew's patent was revoked, the light was extinguished (permanently) and the lighthouse demolished. It was not to be rebuilt until 1752.

Perhaps at this point the opposition of Trinity House should be explored further. As ever, political and financial issues were to the fore. In order to retain their near monopoly on local (Thames) navigation by the provision of pilots, a guild of mariners petitioned Henry VIII in 1513 for a Royal Charter as 'it would be dangerous to allow foreigners, including the Scots, Flemmings and the French, to learn the secrets of the King's streams'. This was granted and in 1514 the guild became known as the Brotherhood of Trinity House and Deptford Strond. Based at the Royal Dockyard at Deptford, the Brethren of Trinity House were to collect all the dues of pilotage on the Thames. So initially Trinity House was in the business of selling its expertise to protect vessels on the Thames, *not* in the fostering of private lighthouses, which just might afford vessels a different type of protection, which might catch on – to the Brethren's financial disadvantage. No less a personage than Samuel Pepys, Master of the Brotherhood in 1607, approved the decision of the Elder Brethren to refuse to allow a light to be established on the Goodwin Sands as it would result in shipmasters not paying for pilotage. He considered lighthouses to be a burden on trade.

Charles II, on the restoration of the monarchy, saw the building of lighthouses as a good way of rewarding his supporters and granted patents to private individuals who, in consultation with Trinity House, were to establish private lights, and of course take levies. For the next two centuries this policy of decentralisation continued with Trinity House sanctioning the building of all lighthouses on any part of the British coast. It was only in 1836, following complaints by ship owners of exorbitant dues, and lighthouses that were not fit for purpose, that 'private lights' were abolished by Act of Parliament. Trinity House was empowered to buy up all the existing lighthouses and given full responsibility for lighthouse construction and development in England, Wales, Gibraltar and the Channel Islands.

This Act only increased the burden placed on Trinity House. At the time of the Act there were few men on the Board with the scientific knowledge to develop lighthouse technology. The English tried-and-trusted approach was simple: build a big tower, put a lot of lamps in it (126 oil lamps at Lowestoft) and use reflectors (4,000 mirrors at Lowestoft) to generate the beam. This approach was completely out of date. While the Brethren of Trinity House had been plodding on in years of complacency, those crafty Frenchmen had developed a revolutionary approach based on optical science. Reflectors actually dissipated and attenuated the light source. The French, guided by the pioneering work of Fresnel, were using refracting lenses to concentrate the beam and their scientists were well funded by the French government (how unfair). Business and manufacturing were also involved and in short the French were, one could say, light years ahead. As we will see, the building and development of Trevose Head lighthouse was part of the fightback.

The tower of St Eval church.

On the north Cornwall coast in those earlier times, the only 'mark' for early mariners was the St Eval church tower which collapsed in 1727 Its importance can be gauged by the fact that the merchants of Bristol and ship owners contributed half the cost of its restoration. In 1829, the Padstow Harbour Association for the Preservation of Life from Shipwreck caused to be built the first coastal 'mark'. The daymark, situated at Stepper Point to mark the entrance to the estuary, and still standing today, is 254ft above sea level, visible from 24 miles out at sea. (The work of the Harbour Association is fully detailed in *Wrecks and Rescues around Padstow's Doom Bar* by this author.)

One man who would not have welcomed the lighthouse – or any other aid to shipping – was the legendary 'wrecker of Trevose', Tom Parsons. His cottage still stands on Booby's Bay and looks down on the rusting remains of the *Karl* of Hamburg, a 1,993-ton steel ship, believed to be a former German minelayer, which broke tow and

An aerial shot of the daymark on Stepper Point. (Peter Chapman)

The *Karl* of Hamburg stranded in Booby's Bay, 1917. (Padstow Museum)

The *Karl* as she is today; an added attraction for holidaymakers.

beached on Constantine on 17 October 1918. Its spectacular skeleton is still visible after certain scouring tides, a tribute to her makers, Ribson & Co. of Maryport (1893). The story goes that a local wrecker (Tom's grandson perhaps?) was seen sneaking on board by a vigilant coastguard. The coastguard clambered up the side of the ship and jumped over the bulwarks only to land on top of the crouching felon who stood up and catapulted the officer overboard. True or false, it is a good tale. It is perhaps ironic, but a sign of the times, that Tom's Cottage is now a holiday let.

Parsons was also credited with luring ships onto the rocks by the use of 'false lights', tying a lantern to his donkey's tail. But in truth all the wrecker had to do was wait for the gale to bring home the booty. On 21 November 1808, the *Integrity* sailing from Quiberon broke from her anchor cables as she was attempting to ride out the gale and beached on Constantine, her crew being rescued by the Padstow cutter *Speedwell*, and on the same morning the sloop *Elizabeth* (Waterford to Shoreham) went to pieces on Treyarnon losing her crew of two. Her cargo of bacon and butter was most welcome to the locals.

Tom Parson's cottage on the path from Constantine Bay to Booby's Bay.

FOR THE WANT OF A LIGHTHOUSE...

'On Monday last,' wrote the *Royal Cornwall Gazette* of 16 November 1811, 'when the vessel came into the breakers, the crew took to their boat which soon filled and melancholy to relate they all drowned. On the following tide the vessel went to pieces and the cargo was lost.' The vessel in question was the *Star*, a brig of 96 tons, sailing from Oporto to Cork with salt and lemons. 'This,' continued the report, 'is another very striking proof of the great necessity for the speedy erection of the proposed lighthouse on Trevose Head, for the want of which many valuable lives and property are continually lost.'

The need for the lighthouse was reiterated by the *Gazette* when a Dutch galliot was wrecked near Padstow on 5 December 1815 with the loss of all her crew:

> Had the so long proposed lighthouse been erected on Trevose Head, it is scarcely to be doubted that this melancholy catastrophe would have been averted, and the lives, ship and cargo preserved. This sad circumstance is another and powerful plea for the immediate erection of the proposed building.

The first recorded application, made through the Admiralty, was submitted in August 1809 by Capt. E. Penrose, and renewed in 1809 by the MPs of the County of Cornwall on behalf of the trade of its ports. In 1815 the *Sherbourne Mercury* reported the 'intention' to make an application to erect a lighthouse.

The years rolled by however and the wrecks and their dead piled up on Trevose and its rocks: the *Concord*, 1821; the *Pearl*, 1823; the *Lyme Packet*, 1824; the *Francis*, 1824; the *Fly*, 1832; the *Agenoria*, 1835; the *Brilliant*, 1841; lost with all hands. The *Gazette* thundered its message:

> It is an extraordinary circumstance that the merchants at Lloyds, who are so deeply interested and must every year have suffered materially for the want of a lighthouse on Trevose Head do not exert themselves and their interests with the Trinity Board and get it done, which would be the means of preventing not merely the numerous losses they sustain in their property by the wrecks but will be the means of saving valuable lives.

Finally in July 1843 the Trinity House authorities instructed their steamer *Vestal*, with Sir Henry Pelley, Deputy Master of Trinity House, on board, to sail up the northern coast and survey the area round Trevose Head with the intention to place a lighthouse there. This mission, as Cyril Noall tells us, was a tragic one. Whilst the steamer waited offshore, two of the Elder Bretheren took a boat to the shore but on returning the boat was taken on a strong tide under the *Vestal*'s bow and capsized. The two dignitaries drowned but the remainder were saved.

The rocks of Bedruthan Steps where the *Samaritan* came to grief in 1846.

But no action was forthcoming, so the sea engineered a few more reminders. In the severe gale of October 1843 the *Hope*, the *Ceres*, the *Leititia*, and the *Wildberforce* were wrecked on the coast. 'The losses occasioned by every succeeding severe gale of wind, shows the necessity of a lighthouse to point out to mariners their situation and prevent their getting into bays from which they can seldom work out again' (RCG). During May 1844 a petition was prepared at Penzance to be forwarded to Trinity House 'praying that the Hon Body to cause a lighthouse to be erected on Trevose Head, near Padstow' (*Penzance Gazette*, 22 May). The authorities still procrastinated (or probably said they would do it 'drekly'?) but a plan was submitted in November 1844 and approved in February 1845.

As work was beginning on the approach road, the last, and most celebrated wreck occurred, that of the *Samaritan* of Liverpool bound for Constantinople, wrecked at Bedruthan Steps on 22 October 1846 with the loss of eight of her crew of ten. She was loaded with all manner of goods: cotton and calico, as well as copper, iron and tinplate. The *Samaritan*, 'the good Samaritan', brought a great bounty to the inhabitants of the surrounding parishes:

> The Good Samaritan came ashore
> To feed the hungry and clothe the poor
> With barrels of beef and bales of linen
> No poor soul shall want for a shilling.

The *West Briton* put it a little more starkly, 'her cargo was then scattered all along the shore at Bedruthan and hundreds of locals gathered on the beach to plunder. Customs and coastguard officers as well as a Lloyds agent attempted to stop the looting and some fifteen men were placed in custody, given sentences of one to four months' and worse, 'it was lamentable that there should be found among these miserable wretches men who stand up in the pulpit to preach the word of God.'

Another local bard used his verses, 'On the loss of the *Good Samaritan* of Liverpool which was unfortunately wrecked on St Eval Cliff on the night of 22 October 1846' to make a further political statement about the much awaited lighthouse:

> Each mother cries, 'Your father's gone.
> Who will for us provide?'
> While soothing friends perhaps may say,
> 'The Lord will that decide'

> Oh! Heavy news for owners too
> And merchants 'tis indeed
> Perhaps they've lost their very all
> With nought to serve their need

But had the Lighthouse been complete
The time it was begun
Eight precious lives might have been saved
And 'Good Samaritan'

May tradesmen on that fabric all
Their time quite well employ
And may they on that structure raise
The topmost stone with joy

And soon the spacious lantern place
On that stupendous pile
With brilliant light, a guide for ships
That in this channel toil

The which I trust will wrecks prevent
That we may hear no more
Of lives being lost or vessels wrecked
In pieces on our shore

Figurehead of the Samaritan.
(Padstow Museum)

THE LIGHTHOUSE AT LAST

We build on firmer base, with loftier hope
The granite shell sits broader on the rock
The light will search the sea with larger scope
And tenfold beam. All mists that veil and mock,
All winds and tides that baffle, shoals that shock
Must yield them to the giant lenses might,
Which flash their splendours soon across the waste of night.

James Kenward
Manager of Chance Lighthouse Works
Birmingham

Trevose Head lighthouse, standing 27m high and visible from 20 miles, was opened on
1 December 1847. The tower was of an unusual design, having two concentric walls in
its upper part with a 2in space between. There was no explanation of this feature and
one can only assume it would be for insulation. The outer wall was 4ft 2½in thick at the

base narrowing to 2ft 8½in at the top. True to the Trinity House tradition, the light was an oil lamp backed by six reflectors. But as Trinity House itself commented: 'The area… is constantly threatened by sea mists that make even the most powerful lights seem like candles.' This makes it difficult to understand why a fog signal was not installed at that time. Prior to 1882 there were two fixed white lights; the high light in the tower and in front of this a low light, which was put in place in June 1847 in order that Trevose should not be mistaken for another lighthouse. The high light burned at an elevation of 204ft above the high water mark, the low light was at an elevation of 129ft and placed 50ft to seaward of the tower. The tower light could be seen from 19 miles and the low light from 16 miles. Dwellings for the lighthouse keepers and their families were built. The total building cost was £7,331 4s 6d. In 1861 Trevose had two keepers paid £65 and £45 per annum.

The problem for ship's masters now was to identify which light belonged to which lighthouse. The *Emile Marie* drove ashore on Constantine Bay on 18 November 1850. Having mistaken Trevose Light for Lundy, the skipper hoped to run under its lee for shelter. He lost four of his six crew in the wreckage. In 1882 the low light was removed, as the identification of Trevose still seemed unsatisfactory, and an occulting (flashing) light was placed in the tower. James Douglas, Supt., recorded his inspection of 31 August 1881 thus:

> Inspected the High Light apparatus after alterations and additions. An intermittent light with 3 occultations in quick succession every minute as follows; light 45 seconds, eclipse 3 seconds, light 3 seconds, eclipse 3 seconds, light 3, eclipse 3; total duration 60 seconds. Tested the apparatus and found all satisfactory completed for exhibition. The light is now exhibited (time 7p.m.) and the machinery is keeping perfect time, everything connected with the change is quite satisfactory – as the night is foggy I have given instructions to light the six wicks.

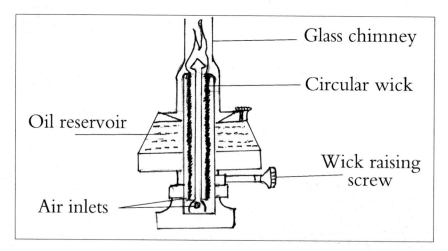

The Argand 'Smokeless' Lamp, used in all Trinity House lighthouses from 1789. The air was drawn up the centre of the wick into the flame. (Drawn from Chance and Williams, 2008)

Old postcard of Trevose lighthouse. (Padstow Museum)

Aerial shot of Trevose lighthouse. (Peter Chapman)

A close-up of Lord Rayleigh's magnificent foghorn. (Padstow Museum)

Perhaps the most celebrated addition to the lighthouse's armoury was the largest foghorn ever installed in an English lighthouse. The enormous trumpet 36ft long with an aperture of 18ft by 2ft must have been an awesome sight to behold and even more daunting to hear at close quarters. Its shape was designed to give a wide horizontal spread of sound. The horn gave two blasts, short – long, every ninety seconds. It was the brainchild of Lord Rayleigh, scientific advisor to Trinity House from 1869 to 1919. The foghorn was put into service on 6 February 1913 and remained so until 1963 when it was replaced by a Supertyphon with eight horns. (But what an attraction it would be for today's coastpath walkers?)

During further modernisation in 1912–13 the light was changed to red flashing every five seconds and in 1920 the Hood vaporised oil burner, developed by David Hood, Chief Engineer of Trinity House, was installed. The light gave out 198,000 candle power with a range of 25 miles. Trevose Head became the first lighthouse to be fitted with the Autoform mantle, one which formed itself into a sphere when burning, overcoming the fragility of previous designs. Even with developments in electrical lighting, oil remained the fuel of choice right up to 1930 when lighthouses went electric. In 1995 Trevose Head lighthouse was automated and the keepers withdrawn. The light, a 35-watt metal halide lamp of 89,000 candelas, reverted to white, flashing every seven seconds. The fog signal is controlled by a fog detector, and in keeping with the modern age (but not as romantic) the operation is controlled and monitored from the Trinity House Operations Centre at Harwich.

The lighthouse with foghorn. (Padstow Museum)

CHAPTER 2

SHIP LOSSES 1700–1914

The ideal seaman is he who says and does the proper thing in the proper way at the proper time, a man who has developed sea sense and nautical sagacity. But ideal conditions and the ideal man seldom, if ever, confront each other in an emergency at sea.

Preface: Nicholls's *Seamanship and Nautical Knowledge.*

In 1752, a sailing ship called the *Margaret* foundered off Trevose. Nothing is known of her or the fate of her crew. What is recorded is that her intended journey was from Bristol to Guernsey. In 1770 the *Elizabeth* was lost 4 miles off Trevose. Her intended passage was London to Dublin. Both these vessels met similar fates off Trevose. We have no record of the reason for their loss but, examining similar incidents, we can surmise that once either vessel cleared the shelter of land they were driven east before the full force of an Atlantic gale and, in attempting to prevent destruction on the coast, missed stays and were swamped.

The *Amiable Anna* foundered in similar fashion in 1815. She was sailing from Ribadeo (Spain) to London. So what was this unfortunate lady doing in Cornish waters? Again we can say that she was either blown north away from her intended course up the Channel, or mistook the coast of Cornwall for the coast of France. If a ship was sailing before a gale, in heavy weather, with no opportunity to take a sighting from the sun by quadrant, then the master had a stark choice: either he could heave to and ride out the blast, putting more time on his voyage, or run on and end up where the wind took him – heading for the iron shore of Trevose.

The major navigational problem for captains in the early days of sail was a simple one. On the open ocean they did not know exactly where they were. Latitude, derived from the fixed lines circling the globe parallel to the equator, could be easily calculated from the height of the sun or known stars above the horizon – always providing of course that these bodies were visible. The calculation of longitude confounded science for centuries until Harrison produced his friction-free clocks in 1773 paving the way for

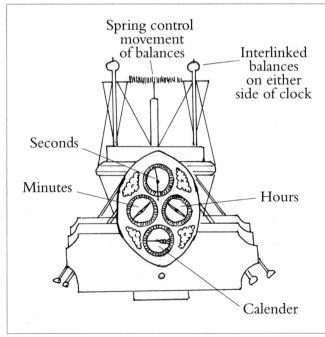

Spring control
movement
of balances

Interlinked
balances
on either
side of clock

Seconds

Minutes

Hours

Calender

Above: The sailor's friend:
the sextant. (Wikimedia
Commons)

Left: Harrison's H1 Sea
Clock. It weighed 76lb
and was tested on a voyage
from Lisbon to England
and proved accurate.
(Drawn from Sobel and
Andrews, 1998).

50.55N
05.40W

1 PANJA ELEUSA 1851

2 RAINBOW

3 FORTUNE 1817

4 ARIAL 1853

5 MARY CAMPBELL 1867

6 JILT 1908

7 ASTERIAS 1870

8 EMILE MARIE 1850

9 LOUISA 1884

10 ALBERT 1859

11 PERSEVERANCE 1914

12 EDIT 1899

13 ZOUAVE 1882

14 JOSEPH & MARIE 1891

15 MARGUERITE-ZELONDIDE 1878

16 PROVIDENCE 1797

17 VENUS 1911

18 ERNEST 1897

19 LEILA 1886

20 ELECTRIC FLASH 1868

21 LA BARROUERE 1897

22 SAM WELLER 1907

23 BERNARD BARTON 1899

24 BREAK OF DAY 1885

25 WESTWARD HO

26 BOSWEDDEN 1886

27 WESTERN MAID 1897

28 LONDON 1820

29 MISTELTOE 1905

30 INDUS 1886

31 AEOLUS 1886

32 IRIS 1852

33 TRADER 1858

34 ACTIVE 1867

35 GALATAEA 1880

36 SAINTE MARIE 1882

37 BESSIE JANE 1881

38 HOME BAY 1890

39 GRACE TOWN 1888

40 UNITY 1896

41 CITY OF EXETER 1888

42 WILLIAM & ANN 1863

43 SUSAN 1865

44 LEADER 1878

45 TRUE BLUE 1860

50.50N

50.45

50.40N

50.35N

44 ⚓

50.30N
05.40W

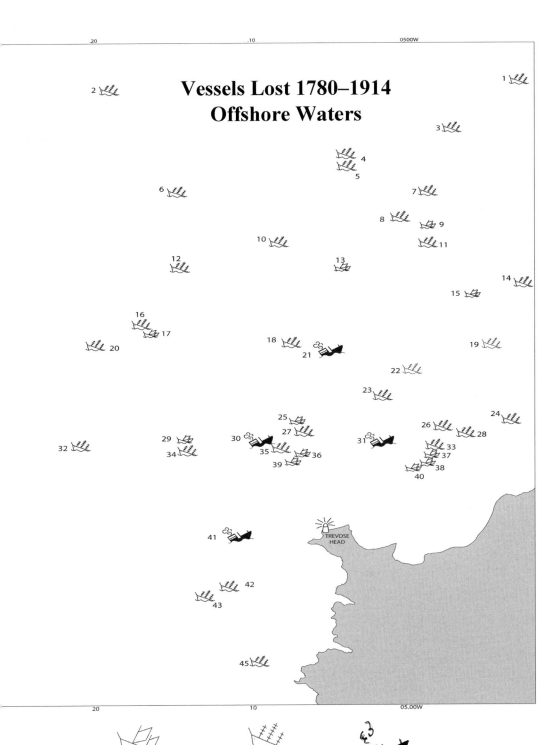

Vessels Lost 1780–1914
Offshore Waters

Fore-Aft rigger   Square rigger   Steam

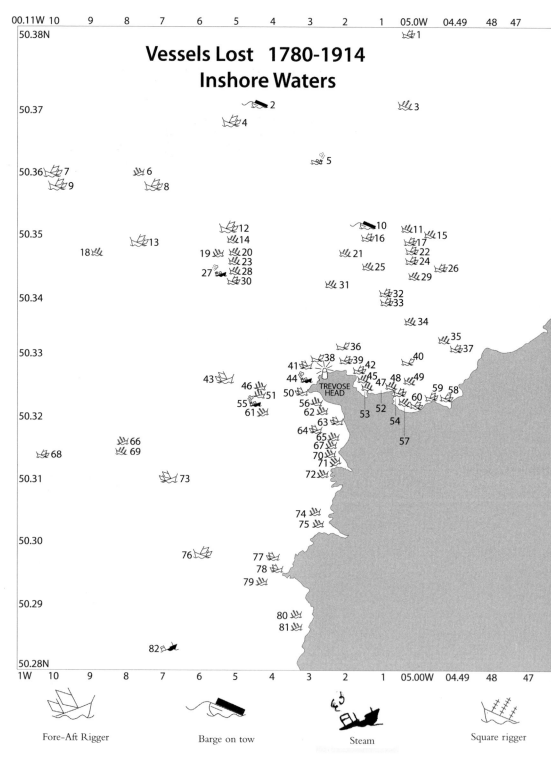

Vessels Lost 1780-1914
Inshore Waters

Fore-Aft Rigger

Barge on tow

Steam

Square rigger

TWO BROTHERS 1811
SHAH 1907
THOMAS AND JANE 1829
CORONATION 1868
SICILIA 1895
THERMUTHIS 1876
PARAAGON 1876
HENRY 1886
DEVONHIA 1904
0 AAD 1895
1 BRILLIANT 1846
2 NATHALIE 1911
3 HANNAH LOUISA 1879
4 IRON AGE 1859
5 CAROLINE 1862
6 PRIDE 1860
7 BETSEY 1815
8 VANITY 1843
9 SUPERIOR 1871
0 TARTAR 1826
1 GERTRUDE 1862
2 DOLPHIN 1815
3 DEVITZ 1869
4 MARY ANN 1833
5 ELIZA & ANN 1863
6 MARY 1816
7 COUNTESS EVELYN 1894
8 TALBOT 1875
9 VOLUNTEER 1865
0 MARY ANN 1876
1 MARIA 1897
2 JOSEPHINE 1874
3 CREOLE 1874
4 PENGUIN 1870
5 MANLY 1845
6 MALPAS 1833
7 PEARL 1884 & ELLIE MARIE 1846
8 RICHARD & ELIZABETH 1859
9 ELIZABETH 1770
0 STAR 1811
1 ALICE 1859

42 CHERIE 1858
43 MARY 1797
44 E.S. LANCASTER 1894
45 GRACE DARLING 1882
46 ROYAL ALBERT 1886
47 FRANCIS 1823
48 INDUSTRY 1912
49 MAI DE DIOS 1782
50 BELT 1906
51 CAROLINE 1867
52 VIKING 1872
53 L'AMELIE 1824
54 MARGARET 1752
55 WHINFIELD 1901
56 REGINA 1854
57 CAROLINA 1768
58 MARIA 1880
59 THREE BROTHERS 1775
60 CATHERINE & ANN 1795
61 EMILIE MARIE 1850
62 MARY 1859
63 JESSIE McCLEW 1895
64 AGENORIA 1835
65 SARAH 1850
66 LIZZIE MALE 1877
67 ST GEORGE 1768
68 AVON 1823
69 THERMUTHIS 1876
70 INTEGRITY 1808
71 VITORIA 1869
72 MARY SPROAT 1891
73 SAINTE MARIE 1914
74 PETREL 1886
75 JAMES ALEXANDER 1860
76 KITTY 1851
77 ENGINEER 1897
78 SPARTAN 1846
79 FULL RIGGER 1859
80 CONCORD 1820
81 SAMARITAN 1846
82 SIRACUSA 1897

The *Amanda* of Padstow, a sloop, an example of the traditional 'fore and aft rigged' ship. Other fore and aft riggers were smack, cutter, ketch and schooner. They carried large sails and a small crew.

The *Maria Assumpta*, was the oldest square-rigged vessel afloat until her tragic loss off Padstow in 1995. Square riggers split up the sails into greater numbers and needed bigger crews. Other square riggers were barques, barquentines, brigs, briganteens, snows, clippers and full riggers.

A practice 'mast' for the Breeches Buoy on Trevose Head.

chronometers and the declaration of the zero meridian at Greenwich in 1884. Sailors sailed roughly on an east or west parallel course and trusted that they would reach their destination. Sometimes the 'destination' loomed up suddenly out of the sea and took them by surprise.

No less a person than Sir Francis Drake must have been rather taken aback in 1586 when he set off from Cartagena to Cuba and arrived sixteen days later at – Cartagena, as a result of navigational errors and compass variation. Closer to home, the loss of the fleet of five 'first rate' ships, *Association*, *St George*, *Eagle*, *Firebrand* and *Phoenix*, by Admiral of the Fleet, Sir Cloudesley Shovell on The Scillies in 1707 was the most celebrated example of misnavigation. It is also related that one unfortunate seaman who had the courage to tell Shovell that by his own (unofficial) calculations, they were some 40 miles off course, was hanged on the spot for insubordination. Legend has it that Sir Cloudesley survived the disaster but having staggered ashore was given a 'good old Cornish welcome' by a lady who clubbed him to death and took the ring off his finger. (Even in more enlightened times the Navy still 'stuck to its guns'. In 1906 HMS *Montague*, engaged in early wireless signalling experiments, ran fast aground in fog on the south of Lundy Island. A landing party walked the length of the island to the North Lundy lighthouse and argued with the keeper that this just *had* to be the Hartland Point lighthouse – damn emmets!)

Historically the maritime fraternity were convinced that as latitude had been correctly forecast by astronomy then the discovery of a correct method for plotting longitude would be derived from the same source. To this end both Louis XIV of France and Charles II had observatories built in Paris (1666) and London at Greenwich (1675). Both sovereigns had obvious interests in establishing secure ocean routes for their expanding trade. In England, a Board of Longitude was set up to offer a cash prize of £20,000 to whoever delivered the goods, and the Astronomer Royal, the Reverend Denis Maskylene, who also happened to be a *de facto* member of the Board, stooped to some rather 'unreverendly' behaviour to try to thwart the 'upstart' Harrison. Harrison was eighty years old when he finally received his prize and it had somehow 'depreciated' to £10,000. (Dava Sobel's book *Longitude* is a must for readers wishing to follow up this aspect of the story.)

The only calculation of longitude available to the mariner was the use of 'the log' to estimate the speed of the ship and thereby distance travelled from home port and from this to an assessment of longitudinal position. The Dutch, it is said, were the first to use the log. A piece of wood was thrown overboard at the bows and the navigator walked aft reciting poetry to see how may verses he could get through by the time the log passed the stern. (Perhaps Cornish sailors sung *Trelawney*?) This 'unsophisticated' method was replaced by tying the log to a line, knotted at seven-fathom intervals and the line paid out against the ship's sand glass. From the number of 'knots' counted over the time, the ship's speed could be calculated.

Of course there were some magnificently daft theories for calculating longitude as often happens when money is at stake. The daftest by far was 'The Wounded Dog

Theory' of 1687. A quack by the name of Sir Kenelm Digby claimed he had discovered a miraculous powder (from deepest southern France) which could cure at a distance. All that needed to be done was to apply this 'Powder of Sympathy' to an article owned by the ailing person. Thus, apply the magic powder to a bandage from a wounded man and *presto*, the wound would close, no matter where the patient was. So, with the thought of lots of money coming his way, the idea was stretched to the solution of the longitude problem. Take a wounded dog on board a ship as she sets sail, leaving ashore a trusted dog handler. At noon the handler ashore was to dip the dog's bandage into the magic powder and the dog, feeling the bandage, would yelp and give the captain the time cue, the yelp indicating that 'the sun is on the meridian at London'. The captain then could compare this 'time-yelp' to the local time on his vessel and calculate the longitude. (You could not make this up!)

Many of the sailing ships that came to grief off north Cornwall during this period were local coasters of low tonnage running coal from Wales to local Cornish ports and beyond to London, Rouen and Elsfleth (Germany) or taking Cornish copper ore to Wales for smelting. In fact the vast majority of vessels lost in this period were heading to or from Welsh ports, necessitating a passage along the north Cornwall coast. On 15 March 1815, the *Betsey* (a very popular name for Cornish brigs), carrying copper ore from Portreath to Wales, sprang a leak and sank. All the crew, save for 'the boy', who was unfortunately left on board, got away in their own boat but it capsized in Constantine Bay and three men were drowned. In similar fashion but further north the ore-carrying *Fortune* (Marazion to Swansea) went down in 1817. On the 'coal run' the schooner *Avon* (Neath to Dartmouth) carrying culm (anthracite) sprang a leak and foundered. The crew of four plus Capt. Tucker got off in the ship's boat and were picked up by the schooner *Richmond*.

The story of the leaking collier that after strenuous bailing eventually sank is recorded over and over again. This is the time before any thought was given to safety at sea – except that which was acceptable to the owner, who in many cases could and did override the skipper. How much a ship should carry and where it should sail, and when, was his decision. However prudent the skipper, there was a business to run and deliveries to be met so there would always be the temptation to carry as much tonnage as possible in vessels of perhaps questionable seaworthiness. The cutter *Josephine* (Cardiff to Newquay) with 87 tons of coal aboard, sank during a gale on 21 August 1894 losing her three crew. The Board of Trade inquiry deemed that she was overloaded and undermanned. The *Josephine* was a mere 37 tons. It was not until the advent of the 'load line' (see later) that there was any idea that sailors should be protected on the job in the same way as any other worker in say a mine or steel works, and in any event many shallow-draft vessels were designed to be beached onshore, loaded up with cargo and floated off on the tide. Many a Padstow craft got into difficulties when loaded by such traditional methods.

Many of these vessels operating out of St Ives, Padstow and Boscastle were elderly ships, second-hand vessels which could be salvaged and rebuilt quite cheaply. The foreign vessels bought were on average sixteen years old. The schooner *Marguerite Selonide*, 98

Paying out the log line. (Nicholls's *Seamanship*)

tons, built in Nantes in 1852 but registered in Penzance in 1878, was on a run from Middlesborough to Newport with pig iron when it foundered 18 miles NNE of Trevose in a heavy sea on 10 July 1878. This vessel was the epitome of the 'coffin ship'. She was twenty-six years of age. She was overloaded. The method of loading her was to line the hold with iron pigs and then the remainder of the pigs were dropped into the vessel until it was full. She leaked. The vessel had begun to leak before it set sail and the leak worsened in a squall to such an extent that the crew eventually abandoned her. The Board of Trade added the inevitable comment that the loss was thought to have been due to such an old vessel labouring under a heavy cargo in a cross sea.

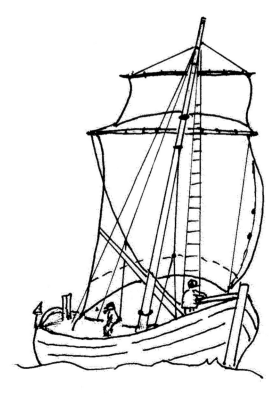

A typical 'collier' of the 1700s taking coal from Wales to Cornwall. How could she withstand the squalls in the Bristol Channel? (Drawn from Bartlett, 1995)

LOSSES BY FOUNDERING

Of the 102 vessels recorded as lost off Trevose, thirty-three were said to have foundered. Now this term may have been used as a universal one to cover any vessel that sank without witnesses, but the idea that a vessel simply 'filled with water and sank', the definition of foundering, is entirely credible. These were in the main small vessels, below 50 tons, which could not stand up to the strain of heavy seas and gale.

Capt. Rayner of the ill-fated HMS *Warwick* gives a graphic description what a squall in the Irish Sea could do to a modern destroyer.

> ... The sky behind me had blackened to an intensity that was appalling. I first saw the line of squall coming down on us at 80 miles per hour. From my reading of old books I was aware of the terrible power of these squalls which could take ships aback and rip the masts out of them. The ship slewed right round and took the wall of foaming water full on her side. I realised that the helmsman had lost control of her and, as she lay right over, I struggled with the wheelhouse door. I got the door open and saw the untended wheel. In the far corner was a muddle of legs and arms which was the helmsman and the bridge messenger. I heard the cry 'Man Overboard'...

It is surprising that not more vessels were recorded as foundered. John Bartlett, in his *Ships of North Cornwall*, lists the average burthen (tonnage) of vessels using the ports in the early trading days:

Portquin	Bude	Port Isaac	Boscastle	Padstow
8 tons	14.5	19.5	21	27.2

He states that tiny Portquin must have sent open boats to Wales for coal and the accompanying illustration of a collier of the time would not have inspired much confidence on the open ocean, and yet still they sailed. In addition, these vessels were designed to be beached for loading with coal or other cargo and floated off at the tide. This was one sure way of finding out if your ship was seaworthy. If she sank, she wasn't.

On 24 November 1852 the *Iris*, a Truro schooner, lost both masts and her bowsprit in a heavy sea 15 miles ESE of Trevose and was recorded by Lloyds as 'swamped'. Fortunately the crew were taken off by the *Honour* of Fowey after she saw their signals of distress. The *Richard and Elisabeth*, a Barnstaple smack of only 16 tons, was unable to bear the might of a Force 9 gale and went down 1 mile from the Head on 26 October 1859. Having taken to their own boat when their vessel *True Blue* of Teignmouth, bound for Chester with zinc ore, foundered on 7 July 1862, a similar distance from Trevose, the crew were fortunate to be towed to Padstow and cared for by Mr Hicks, the agent for the Shipwrecked Mariners Benevolent Society.

The schooner *Superior* (Neath to St Ives), with coal, was running for the shelter of Padstow harbour on 24 August 1871. When she was about 4 miles off Trevose, she was struck by a heavy sea and foundered at 1p.m. The crew barely had time to get into their boat before she sank. They then endured six hours of torment, drifting off the coast and being frequently swamped by heavy seas. Eventually they reached Harbour Cove, Padstow. The Cornish Times reported they had lost all their belongings and one man who had recently been paid off from another ship lost between £7 and £8. This was in his chest which went down with the vessel. Fortunately the boat was insured with the St Ives Shipping Club for £150

Recorded by the Board of Trade inquiry as having 'foundered during the stress of weather' the schooner *Lizzie Male* (Swansea to Fecamp) with coal was seen in difficulties 4 miles off Trevose on 29 January 1877. She had already lost her masts and was showing distress flags. Braving tremendous seas, the Newquay lifeboat, *Pendock Neale*, rowed for two hours to reach the stricken vessel and took off the crew of six plus Capt. Male. The return journey was equally as perilous as it was approaching low water. At one point a lifeboatman was washed overboard but recovered and a sea anchor or drogue was streamed to enable the cox'n to run the lifeboat onto the beach.

On 24 February 1884 Capt. Killgallon of the *Eurydice* of and for St John's with salt and coal from Liverpool put into Newport through stress of weather. He reported an encounter with the schooner *Rover* of Padstow some 35 miles south-west of Lundy. She was in a sinking state with one man dead from exposure. Killgallon stood by for six hours and tried to save the men by throwing lines over; all to no avail in the heavy sea. He then induced four of the *Rover's* crew, by the promise of money, to launch their boat. This they did but could not get near the *Eurydice*. The mate Francis Lawke, of Port Isaac, jumped over to the *Eurydice* and caught its chains and was pulled aboard by the steward. Both captains attempted to throw more lines to the boat and one man got partially on board but his hands were benumbed by the cold and he could not hold on. The vessels separated and the *Rover* sank.

On 3 March 1897, a large steamer was seen in difficulties 5 to 6 miles off the coast below Trevose Head in treacherous weather. It was identified as the *Siracusa*, a 100-ton collier carrying a crew of twenty-four. The Newquay lifeboat *Willie Rogers* immediately put out but could make no headway to the vessel after rowing for three hours. The steamer drifted away with a heavy list to port, probably due to a shift in the cargo, but after firing rockets at 11.30p.m. it disappeared. It foundered with the loss of all hands. The passage of the *Siracusa* was geographically recorded by H. Thomas of Padstow in the opening verses of his poem:

WRECKS AND LOSS OF LIFE ON THE CORNISH COAST

The news that came to Padstow
It was not of the best
There was a steamer below Trevose
And she was in distress

The lifeboat men were summoned
And to their post to stand
The got the Rockets ready
To run along the land

But the steamer went to westward
In all the wind and sea
And they launched the Newquay Lifeboat
And proceeded off to sea

The Newquay lifeboat made a second abortive trip that night to try to reach the Fowey ketch *Engineer* which broke up on Park Head with the loss of its three crew.

LOSSES BY COLLISION

Twenty-seven vessels, recorded lost off Trevose in this early period, were due to a collision of some description with another vessel. (Larne records the astonishing figure of seventy

A merchantman battling a heavy swell. (Hurd)

collisions for the whole of Cornwall in this time.) Sometimes the perpetrator was able to rescue the crew, sometimes she was 'unknown' and sometimes, as in the case of the *Westward Ho*, a Padstow trawler, there was a maritime pile-up. The *Westward Ho* was cut in half by the SS *Picton* 9 miles north of Trevose on 16 April 1909, and then the wreck, or half of it, collided with the ketch *Proceed* of Ramsgate. Three of the crew of five were drowned including the captain, Morris. Frank Strike (1965) in his book *Cornish Shipwrecks*, points out that the waters off Trevose were a very busy thoroughfare 'with sailing coasters and steam colliers flowing past in unbroken procession to and from South Wales'. There was no coastguard radio then to steer them into 'Traffic Separation Schemes' and each skipper would be intent on making the shortest journey to deliver the cargo on time. They would also stick to popular and well-sailed courses. This gives us some insight as to the reasons for the collisions and the accompanying chart attempts to show the major plots of the 'Coal Run'.

However key evidence for the abundance of collisions is given by E. W. Anderson in his book *Man the Navigator*:

Originally the only problem in navigation was to find the way. With the increase in marine trade the number of ships in the main routes began to cause problems. It is a feature of navigation that as soon as a way is found so many people use it that the problems of collision arise. Thus emphasis shifts from finding the way to avoiding collision, and collisions began to assume the nature of a major hazard to navigation.

But why? Surely these experienced skippers could see each other coming?

Anderson continues to surprise us with the fact that it was not until 1862 that 'rules of the road' were agreed between England and France and accepted by the United States in 1864. These rules gave directions as to which of two ships meeting should take avoiding action and under which circumstances a ship should stand on and not alter course, for it was important for the other ship to know when a vessel would keep to its present course. ('Keep to the right' was, of course, a basic rule of river sailing. Derived from the time when the steerboard (rudder) was on the right of the vessel, convenient to the right of the helmsman. It was safer to let ships go by on the left to avoid getting the steerboards tangled. The left side, unencumbered, was the side used for tying the boat up to the quay – so it became the 'port' as opposed to the 'starboard'.)

Anderson further adds another change in the status of navigation; the decline of the captain/navigator. With an increase in marine insurance from 1800 onwards, a large proportion of the risks of voyages were taken on by newly formed limited liability companies. As a result the shipmaster began to be relegated to an employee on a low wage, which in turn caused a decline in the master's skills. The frequency of collisions in proportion to voyages in the first half of the nineteenth century was only reversed when the Navigation Acts – British goods in British ships with British crews – were repealed after 1850, and the industry was forced to compete for contracts making skilled navigation once again essential.

Two trawlers after a fatal collision. (Anderson)

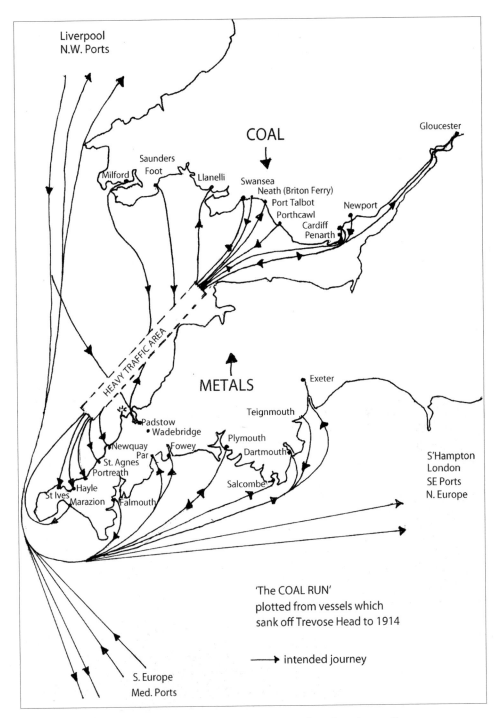

A map of the 'Coal Run'; Cornish metals to Wales and Welsh coal to Cornwall.

Richard Larne adds to our knowledge in his review of the 1836 report by the Select Committee on Shipwrecks. The evidence of this committee, the first ever review of marine management in all its aspects, revealed that the losses over the period of review were staggering: 1.3 ships were lost every day at an estimated cost of £14,525,000 with the loss of 3,414 crew. One hundred and thirty vessels had gone down with all hands and ninety-five ships just vanished. And the reasons?

> The frequent incompetency of masters and officers ... want of skill and knowledge of seamanship ... more frequently want of knowledge of navigation. Some hardly know how to trace a ship's course on a chart ... cannot ascertain latitude ... are unacquainted with the chronometer ... some are appointed to command at periods of extreme youth... one instance is given of a boy of 14, all of whose apprentices were older than himself ... drunkenness ... sleeping on the lookout ... frequently traceable to the intoxicating influence of spirits.

Paul Boissier, an ex-Navy submariner with years of experience, in his book *Rules of the Road*, is a little bit more sympathetic to the modern navigator and his attempts to avoid collision. 'It is frightening when you are the "stand on vessel" (the ship which in theory has the right of way) and you don't know if the other ship has seen you. How long do I maintain my course and speed?' As he says, it is all about individual judgement. He adds his own rule of thumb, 'don't alter to port for a vessel on your port side'. The simple reason being that if you alter to port and he suddenly sees you and grabs his steering control he will always veer to starboard and you will collide. Unfortunately the COLREGS (Collision Regulations) were only published in 1972; not 1772. Boissier also adds a new term to the lexicon, the 'SatNav' collision. Most skippers, now equipped with state-of-the-art location finders, use the same coastal way points to get their bearings with the result that vessels congregate in one spot, increasing the probability of collision.

On 12 November 1848 the stern of a vessel clearly marked *Brilliant* (Hayle to Llanelli with copper ore) was washed into St Ives harbour. The captain of an American barque sailing to Cardiff reported that at 1a.m. that same day he had accidentally run down a deep-laden schooner off Trevose Head. The vessel had gone down so quickly that he could not save the crew who appeared to have perished with the vessel. This event was replicated in the loss of the smack *Kitty* (Charlestown to Liverpool with china clay) and her three crew. Her stern and main boom were towed into Newquay on 22 November 1851. She had been struck on 11 November by the smack *Emma Jane* of Jersey in a SE Force 6 gale.

Some crews were lucky, being picked out of the water by the self-same ship that collided with them. On 10 March 1853 the 48-ton *Malpas* (Rouen to Swansea with copper dross) was struck by the schooner *Ono* of St Ives making a hole so large that she almost sank immediately. One of the crew drowned but the other two clambered on board the *Ono*.

Collisions between sailing ships and the 'newfangled' steamers were more frequent and, unfortunately for the sailing vessel, usually more disastrous, as the century progressed. An Admiralty Court was convened to give judgement in the case of the coal-carrying schooner *Volunteer* of Plymouth run down by the SS *Minerva* at midnight on 11 December 1865. With 134 tons facing a steam-driven 497 tons there could only be one outcome. The schooner sank and five of her seven crew were drowned. The master and the helmsman, reported as being the only crew members who could swim, were picked up by the *Minerva* and taken to Cardiff. The Court, as reported by the Royal Cornwall Gazette, heard that the crew of the *Minerva* had seen the schooner's navigation lights but that the collision had still taken place. The *Minerva's* captain, in his defence, said that when the collision was inevitable he ordered the wheel 'hard a port' and stopped engines. He added that had the sailing vessel taken similar action in changing tack they could have avoided each other. Dr Lushington, passing judgement, said that the blame was entirely due to the negligence of the steamer captain and found for the plaintiff.

When the SS *Edendale* of Sunderland sliced into the 353-ton *Galatea* of Swansea bound from that port to Cape Town with coal on 5 December 1880 causing her to sink forty-five minutes later, 'pure negligence' was the common verdict. The sea was calm, the weather clear and the steamship ran into the barque at full speed, driving 4ft into her port side. She was 10 miles NNW of Trevose Head and the *Edendale* picked up the complete crew of twelve and the captain, James. Unfortunate to relate the ship's dog was left behind on board the sinking vessel.

The *Cornish Times* of 25 September 1884 carried the headline, 'PADSTOW SCHOONER RUN DOWN' and continued:

> Padstow schooner *Mary Josephine*, Pollard master, Penzance–Newport in ballast, was about 15 m north of Trevose Head between 5 or 6 o clock of Sunday morning when the steamer *Ackworth* of West Hartlepool, Capt. Clegg, ran into her. The mishap was caused by the carelessness of the officer on watch on the steamer. The steamship struck the schooner full on the bow. The bow was smashed and the bowsprit and windlass carried away. The crew and the captain's wife making her first voyage had barely time to take to their boat when the vessel went down by the bow. Had she been fully laden all would have perished. They were brought to the entrance to Padstow harbour by the *Ackworth* en route to Port Said and reached Hawker's Cove in their own boat.

Even royalty was not immune to disaster. On 20 August 1875 the Royal Yacht *Alberta* with Victoria herself aboard ran down the *Mistletoe* with the loss of her skipper and a female passenger. Apparently the *Mistletoe* was 'dipping her flag' in deference to the monarch and neglected her helm.

LOSSES BY LEAKING

Putting to sea in an unseaworthy craft was a sailor's nightmare. He signed on in good faith and trusted that the master, who generally owned his own vessel, would not easily risk his personal fortune and his life and had maintained the ship in good order. Yet how was he to know if this ship was one of those 'coffin brigs' deliberately sent out to sea as an 'insurance loss'?

On 2 June 1860 the 49-ton schooner *Pride* (Porthcawl–Exeter) sprang a leak off Trevose and went down so quickly that the crew had to abandon all their belongings and take to their boat. After four hours of rowing they were picked up by the schooner *Aid* on passage to London and transferred to a Falmouth fishing boat off the Manacles. Capt. Bradfield, the Hon. Sec. of the Shipwrecked Mariners Society, took care of the four crew and, after food and rest, sent them to their respective homes in Exeter and Swansea.

The *Coronation*, a 42-ton Bideford smack with coal from Porthcawl to Falmouth, developed a leak 5 miles NW of Trevose and sank at 3p.m. on 15 May 1868. The crew were fortunate to escape in their own boat as were the thirty-one crew of the SS *Indus*, 2,486 tons, which developed a leak 9 miles NW of Trevose sailing with coal from Cardiff to Tenerife. She sank at 5.30a.m. on 14 October 1886, the crew eventually landed at Port Isaac by lifeboat.

On 11 February 1888, the 1,054-ton steamship *City of Exeter* was observed by the master of the *Sarah Ann* to be flying distress signals about 8 miles off Trevose. The steamer signalled 'Will you take me in tow?' As the *Sarah Ann* bore up to the steamer she signalled again, 'We are leaking and the boats are stove.' As the *Sarah Ann*'s crew were preparing their lifeboats they saw the *City of Exeter* roll over and sink. The wind was west Force 10. One crew member was saved, Olisi Morsen, a Norwegian, who was subsequently landed at Lundy.

Added to the list of vessels lost by leaking, must be the SS *Jackal* which 'disappeared somewhere off Trevose Head' on 26 November 1881. This 116-ton ship was on her maiden voyage from Preston to Natal for service in the Blue Anchor Line. She docked at Padstow on 23 November having already been forced to shelter from the gales in Holyhead and Fishguard. Her shape and low freeboard drew criticism from onlookers and her crew, exhausted and seasick, agreed with Capt. Downer, her master, that they would sail to Falmouth for bunkers but no further. She duly left Padstow on 25 November and was seen by the coastguard passing Trevose Head. The next morning she was sighted off St Agnes Head returning up channel looking in good shape. But two days later the wreckage of the *Jackal* littered Constantine Bay. The bodies of the captain and crew were never found. The Board of Trade enquiry (18 January 1882) was faced with conflicting statements. The builder maintained that the ship was strong and the Lloyds surveyor (Liverpool) was of the opinion that she might well have made the trip in safety. The Chief CO in Fishguard thought otherwise and two Padstow men testified that the crew complained about leaking and that the engineers were being drenched by seawater coming down into the engine room.

LOSSES BY FIRE

Abandoning your leaking vessel was preferable to having it blow up beneath you. Ships carrying wood, charcoal, hemp and cotton were particularly vulnerable to fire, especially

A sailing ship on fire: a dramatic painting by the Russian Bogolugov. (W.C.)

wooden-hulled vessels. In colliers, 'fire damp' was just as dangerous as it was in the coal mines themselves. On 30 April 1853, the *Ariel* (Cardiff to Elsfleth, Germany) was sailing west of Trevose on a calm sea. The cabin boy had taken a candle into the hold to inspect the cargo, dropped it, and the naked flame ignited the fire damp. Luckily two of the three crew were picked up by the passing schooner *Illustrious*.

(Human error, i.e. sheer stupidity, played a major part in many of these disasters. The *Washington*, carrying 3,000 bales of cotton, was set ablaze in Falmouth Harbour (23 October 1799) when the cook went into the hold with the ubiquitous 'dropped candle' to look for his knife. The *Georgiana* stranded at Porthoustock (29 August 1871) was set on fire by its own crew who decided to light a distress signal by pouring paraffin on an old sail which ignited her cargo of railway sleepers and burned the ship down to the water's edge.)

A gas explosion disabled the *Asterias*, a barque of 800 tons, sailing with 1,530 tons of coal from Liverpool to Hong Kong on 21 May 1870. The *Royal Cornwall Gazette* tells the story in its inimitable style:

TERRIBLE EXPLOSION AT SEA

The crew which numbered 14 hands all told, consisted of Captain Slone, two officers and 11 coloured seamen. All proceeded well until a quarter to ten on Saturday morning, when, the vessel being at the time 20 miles off Lundy, a fearful explosion took place. Commencing forward, the shock travelled aft, laying open the cargo and stores, the deck parting in the middle, dislodging the bulwarks and stanchions, carrying away portions of the sails and rigging, smashing the boats and throwing the crew in all directions. A coloured man, by the name of John Johnson, who was at the wheel, was blown into the air and never seen again … Another was thrown into the sea but caught a rope and was hauled on board. The captain was found between the main and mizzen masts. Bleeding from mouth and ears he died twenty minutes later. Two men were badly burned, another had a broken thigh and a fourth was scorched. The men threw the long boat overboard and a lifeboat and scrambled in, taking Captain Slone with them. They had no sooner got off when the masts, which had so far stood firmly, together with a portion of the rigging and sails came crashing down on them, threatening them with instantaneous death. They escaped and were picked up two hours later by the briganteen *Success* of Dublin. She arrived in Mounts Bay on Monday morning. Here the twelve survivors took to their boats and were towed to Penzance by the schooner *Beryl*.

The *Paragon* sailing from Milford to Southampton carrying charcoal was gutted by fire 6 miles NW by W off Trevose, on 17 May 1876. The crew got off in the ship's boat and they were towed to Newquay by a French lugger. The *Falcon* of Ipswich on arrival at Falmouth reported that she had passed the *Paragon* on fire 6 miles off Trevose. Everything was burned out but the hull.

The problem of safety on colliers, it seems, was an insurmountable problem. At the Board of Trade inquiry into an explosion on the *Maranda* of Hull (22 September 1875) it was explained that the fire started because of the inadequate ventilation of the cargo but that this was a consequence of battening down the hatches in rough weather, a logical action to prevent the ship from foundering. In addition it was stated that no other means of ventilation existed. The Court returned the master's ticket and exonerated all parties from blame. In similar fashion, the SS *Japanese* of London was towed into Cardiff on 1 November 1882 by a salvage tug, having been gutted by fire in her bunkers near Trevose Head. She was en route for Marseilles from Penarth Roads.

The most spectacular pyrotechnic display afforded to hundreds of spectators gathered on the coast near Boscastle was the destruction of the SS *Londos* carrying petroleum and benzoline in casks, 100 of which were carried on deck. Fire was discovered in the engine room and the vessel was abandoned on 15 November 1891. As each cask of petroleum fell into the sea it burst into flames spreading the fire in all directions.

LOSSES IN FOG

Sea fog, unpredictable in its arrival, and engulfing sailors in a deadening cloak, was, and still is, an ever present hazard on the north coast, causing collisions and unforeseen strandings.

A ship in a fog drift. (M. Zinkova, W.C.)

On 22 September 1884 in dense fog the Padstow ketch *Louisa* was in collision with the SS *Resolute* of Liverpool and sunk with all hands. The *Resolute* could find no trace of the vessel after cruising round the spot for forty minutes and reported the accident on her arrival at Portreath.

The steamship *Countess Evelyne* (Bilbao to Cardiff with iron ore) ran into patches of dense fog off Trevose on 13 May 1893 and later that evening collided with the Dublin-registered SS *City of Hamburg*. The impact was reported as 'slight' on the bow of the *City of Hamburg* and the crew were unaware of the damage the ship had caused. The master of the *Countess Evelyne*, Capt. Evans, ran forward to find out what had happened but his ship went down so quickly that he barely had time to jump onto the deck of the Dublin ship as his own sank beneath him. Of the eighteen crew, sixteen were drowned. The only other survivor was the first officer, who at the time of the collision was asleep in his bunk and had the good fortune to be able to scramble through the hole made in the side of the ship. The SS *City of Hamburg* lowered three boats but found only a young girl passenger already dead and a seaman named Jardine who died soon after. The *City of Hamburg* was 1,219 tons, the *Countess Evelyne* 864.

In the following year the steamship *ES Lancaster* (Newhaven to Cardiff in ballast) struck Trevose Head in dense fog at 3a.m. on 11 October and sank leaving her masts visible just above the water. Part of the crew got off in their own boat and the rest were picked up by the lifeboat.

The worst job in the Navy: a forward lookout exposed to the elements peers through the fog on this destroyer. (Hurd)

LOSSES BY ABANDONMENT

The specific charge of loss by abandonment or rather 'reckless abandonment' was brought against Capt. Corbines, master of the brig *Thermuthis*, a 229-ton vessel carrying coal from Cardiff to Demerara in October 1876. It was alleged, and subsequently upheld, that 'on the 12 October last he did feloniously, unlawfully and maliciously cast away and destroy a certain brig or vessel called the Thermuthis, the property of Fred W. Baddeley and others of Brixham'.

The actual events seem very like many of the other sinkings. The vessel developed a leak, and was abandoned off Trevose at 4a.m., the crew taking to their own boat and landing at Trevose Bay. Five minutes later she struck the rocks and broke up. Obviously there was more to it than the reported events suggest and Corbines had his certificate suspended by the Board of Trade.

LOSSES ON THE QUIES

The 'Quies' are a series of islets which stand a mile west of Trevose Head, waiting in eight fathoms to rip the bottom out of any misguided vessel. The *Royal Albert*, a full rigger of 1,438 tons, sailing from Calcutta to Liverpool with a cargo of tea, cotton bales, castor oil and India rubber struck, on 17 January 1866, came off and sank in deep water. There was no trace of her thirty-four crew or of Capt. Davies. Much of the cargo was recovered from the wreck which was insured for £160,000.

The Quies were waiting for the schooner *Caroline* in the following year 1867, on 11 October. This unfortunate vessel had been windbound in Padstow on its journey from Newport to Salcombe with coal and was at last passing Trevose Head with every hope of completing her voyage. The crew had just gone below leaving the mate at the helm. He was instructed that he could either pass inside or outside the Quies. As often happened in the days of sail his choice, to pass inside, proved fatal. The wind suddenly fell to a dead calm and taken on the ebb tide the *Caroline* struck the rocks and broke up. Fortunately the crew got away in their own boat and made it back to Padstow.

The combination of the Quies and dense fog put paid to the 1,468-ton steamship *Whinfield* on 24 April 1901. She was coming back to Cardiff with iron ore from Decido when she struck and foundered in heavy seas. The crew were fortunate to be picked up by a Barry pilot cutter and towed into Padstow by the tug *Active*.

Left: The Quies rocks off Trevose Head.

Below: The Quies from Booby's Bay; left foreground is an exposed spar from the *Karl* of Hamburg.

LOSSES BY BREAKING ANCHOR/TOW

In an attempt to combat the heavy seas many vessels dropped anchor, usually more than one, in the hope of riding out the storm. Some were unsuccessful.

On 21 November 1808 the *Integrity* sailing from Quiberon (with Cornforth as master) was caught in a violent gale off Trevose blowing dead onshore. Not being able to clear the land she cut away her masts and rode out the gale until the following day (Sunday) when her cables parted and she was driven onshore and was dashed to pieces. Fortunately for the crew the cutter *Speedwell* under Capt. Hopkins had come out from Padstow and took them into the port.

The *Penguin*, a St Ives schooner of 80 tons, was reported to have 'disappeared' from Mother Ivey's Bay after having anchored in a gale on 12 October 1870. Her crew left her at anchor, landing in the ship's boat. But on the following day she had gone – presumed foundered.

The *Hannah Louise*, a 56-ton trow from Gloucester to Padstow with coal, was put ashore by her captain, Wheatstone, who mistook Perranporth for Padstow. The following day, 2 August 1879, she was discharged and refloated. The Padstow tug *Amazon* took her in tow at 6p.m. with the original crew of four on board plus four other men to assist at the pumps. As the vessels were passing Trevose Light with a west wind and an ebb tide running at eight knots, there were cries from the trow and as the *Amazon* dropped back to investigate the sailer was seen to give a sudden lurch and went down bow first. Lines were thrown to the men in the water but two, Oliver Warzan and Thomas Glason, were drowned. The subsequent Board of Trade inquiry found her to have been unseaworthy.

LOSSES BY NAVIGATION ERROR

On 17 November 1850, a chasse marie from Sarzeau (France), the *Emile Marie*, with coal from Liverpool to Bordeaux, drove ashore on the west of Trevose Head at 10p.m. and became a total wreck. Four crew, including the master, Capt. Carhoalent, lost their lives. The two survivors stated that they had mistaken Trevose Head light for Lundy and had attempted to run under its lee or shelter. The body of a lad, thought to be one of the crew, was washed ashore and buried in St Merryn parish.

Navigational error on a grand scale led to the loss of the *James Alexander*, a 1,089-ton full rigger which sailed from Liverpool bound for Calcutta with a cargo of salt. She left her home port on 18 January 1860, Capt. Atcock taking his wife aboard as a passenger. Having run down the St Georges Channel and sighted Tuskar Rock on 19 January, the ship ran into heavy gales which meant that her position at noon on 20 January was by dead reckoning. On 21 January the Old Head of Kinsale was sighted but at 6p.m. she was stuck by heavy seas which did considerable damage. Capt. Atcock then decided to head back for Tuskar Rock, when a light was spotted 12 miles distant. The chief officer expressed the view that he thought it was Trevose Light, but the master continued to run in to what he thought was Milford Haven. As land was sighted, the mistake was quickly realised but the crew were unable to get sufficient sail on in time to ward off the inevitable. She ran ashore 3 miles west of Trevose Head under St Eval Cliff, but of the twenty-seven crew, only one man was lost, apparently a victim of disobedience of the captain's orders.

Perhaps Capt. Stone of the fishing vessel *Renown*, was the 'worse for wear' on 10 March 1903 when he was sailing back to Padstow with his night's catch. Rounding what he thought was Trevose lighthouse, he suddenly discovered he was stranded on rocks at Newquay. What he had just passed were the lights of the Headland Hotel. He ordered his crew to abandon ship. Four of his crew got to safety but sad to record a boy cook named Angus, who was afraid to jump across to the rocks, slipped into the sea and was drowned.

LOSS BY DELIBERATE OVERLOADING

After a long and seemingly endless campaign against ship owners and statesmen, Samuel Plimsoll, MP for Sheffield, 'the sailors friend', saw his load line, ever after known as the Plimsoll Line, become law in 1875. (Nicolette Jones' most excellent book *The Plimsoll Sensation* tells the story.) As with the 'lighthouse debate' it would appear that no one in power supported the idea that the load carried by a ship should actually be regulated by statute. This seemed to strike at the very heart of the free-born English mariner – not to mention the pockets of the free-born English merchant! The deadly game that the more unscrupulous owners played was to load the vessel until it just about made way and insure the vessel and cargo for loss. A 'win-win' situation for them and 'lose-lose' for the sailors and their bereaved families. Witness a letter of March 1867 from the owner of the vessel *Utopia* to the replacement captain who objected, as had his predecessor, to sailing the overloaded vessel to India:

> I am very much surprised to hear that you are making difficulties about going in the Utopia. And I must inform you that if you do not go out in the vessel, I will take care you never get employment in a ship out of this port (Liverpool) if I have the power to prevent you!

The captain climbed down, the unfortunately named *Utopia* sailed with over 3ft of water in the hold and sank. The owner, of course, collected the insurance. In a comment on the disaster the RNLI recommended two remedies for this discreditable state of things: an independent inspection of ships and a 'thin white line' showing the legally binding level to which they should be loaded. As would be expected – nothing was done.

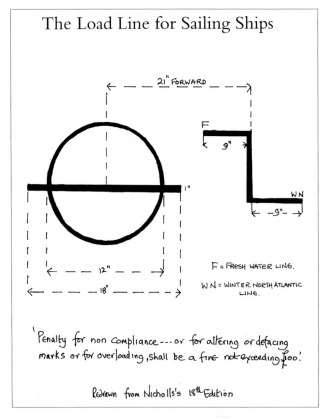

The Load Line for Sailing Ships

21" FORWARD

F

9"

1"

WN

9"

12"

18"

F = FRESH WATER LINE.

WN = WINTER NORTH ATLANTIC LINE.

'Penalty for non compliance --- or for altering or defacing marks or for overloading, shall be a fine not exceeding £100'.

Redrawn from Nicholls's 18th Edition

Left: The sailor's saviour: the Plimsoll Load Line. (Nicholls's Seamanship)

Below: The *Industry*, a collier stranded on Harlyn Bay on 27 September 1912 and broken up. (Padstow Museum)

Above: The *Jessie McClew*, a collier stranded on Booby's Bay on 2 October 1895. (Padstow Museum)

Below: A cannonball, possibly from HMS *Bloodhound*, wrecked in Harlyn Bay in 1811. (Padstow Museum)

This cannon ball was found in the sand at Bloodhound Cove, Harlyn Bay. It probably came from "H.M.S. BLOODHOUND" which was wrecked there in December 1811, whilst engaged in protecting convoys from French privateers. Eleven crew members drowned.

The loss of the *Indus*, which foundered in heavy seas off Trevose Head, reported in the *Cornish Times* of October 1886, was a typical example of an overloaded vessel. The Board of Trade inquiry found that, 'her great length and small beam and the great depth to which she was loaded, sufficiently explained the large quantities of water she took in as the wind shifted. Considerable blame is attached to the captain, loading the vessel deeper than the Lloyds certificate warranted.' The *Cornish Times* was however, in an earlier edition, somewhat disparaging of Board of Trade inquiries: 'It would be well to stop the wasteful expense of some of these investigations and apply the savings to improvements in the harbours of Padstow and Newquay!'

Unfortunately, unscrupulous men will always find ways and means to bend the law. On 28 November 1882, the steamship *St George*, on the 'coal run' from Swansea to Nantes, ran into heavy weather off the Cornish coast. As the gale built up to Force 10, the heavy seas breaking over the decks ripped away the tarpaulins covering the after hatch and water poured into the vessel. The boat began to settle lower and lower into the water and the captain, MacKean, ordered one of her boats to be got ready. Seven fortunate crew members got into it but suddenly the *St George* foundered, leaving all ten of the remaining crew and a passenger to go down with the ship.

The *Petrel*, stranded in Wine Cove on 9 December 1886, where it broke up. (D. Lindsay)

Salvaging blocks of marble from the *Petrel*, sold to the salvors for £5. (D. Lindsay)

The resulting Board of Trade inquiry found that the boat was too deeply loaded, especially in the stern. The *St George* was a 500-tonner and was carrying 525 tons of coal in two holds with 200 tons of copper ingots in the after hold. It was revealed that the owner of the vessel had (illegally) raised the load line and loaded the vessel down to it leaving only 18in of freeboard. He had also taken control of the cargo loading himself, overriding his skipper. Mrs MacKean, the captain's widow, had booked a passage on the ship but, exercising a woman's common sense, got off at Bristol – she said the ship was overloaded.

Winching the blocks of marble up the cliff: The seated figure must be the Clerk of Works. (D. Lindsay)

CHAPTER 3

1914–18:
THE U-BOAT MENACE

'We arise, we lie down
And we move
In the belly of death.
The ships have a thousand eyes
To mark where we come
But the mirth of a seaport dies
When our blow gets home'

Rudyard Kipling 'Tin Fish', 1914-18

The First World War brought a terrifying enemy to the waters off Trevose – the German *Unterseeboot*, or U-boat. Of the seventy-one vessels lost there, sixty-four were destroyed by torpedo, gunfire or scuttling. Yet at the start of hostilities the submarine was considered a nautical curiosity of uncertain usefulness. For many, such warfare was the height of treachery and cowardice – attacking a fellow's ship without being seen was just not on. Indeed the first German submarine war patrol in January 1914 from Heligoland was a disaster. One of the U-boats ran into a mine, another fired off all its (expensive) torpedoes and missed every target, another, *U-15*, was rammed and sunk (by the cruiser *Birmingham*) and another was trapped on the surface with mechanical troubles. It seemed that the joke was on 'Kaiser Bill', especially as in the all important 'real' vessel count Britain had far more Dreadnought battleships; nineteen to Germany's thirteen.

Then things changed. The cruiser *Pathfinder* was torpedoed and sunk with 259 crew lost in September 1914, followed later in the same month by the torpedoing of the cruisers *Aboukir*, *Cressy* and *Hogue*, one after the other, by *U-9*, under Otto Weddigen, with a total loss of 1,460 sailors. Even this German success was accompanied by the teething troubles of the submarine. Each time the *U-9* boat fired a torpedo, the bows lifted and broke the surface of the water due to the displacement of weight. To counter this, Weddigen had his crew dashing forward to the bows with each shot, as mobile ballast, to maintain the U-boat's trim. Nonetheless the loss of three of 'Britannia's finest' shocked the nation.

Above: A German U-boat of 1914; the scourge of the seas. (Hurd)

Left: A lithograph of the *U-9* returning to base in triumph after sinking three British battleships. (Navy Photos, W. C.)

An all-too-familiar sight: a U-boat crew survey their kill. (Carl Bossenroth, W.C.)

Press and public could not believe that this was all the work of one submarine. The Navy, having, rather stupidly, disbanded its anti-submarine warfare committee when the war began, naturally were rather worried. Anti-submarine detection did not exist. Lake (2006) tells us that the Navy's initial response was to use a patrol of anti-submarine picket-boats armed with '... a canvas bag and a hammer. When a periscope appeared our gallant boys were to put the bag over it and smash the glass with the hammer.'

Initially the legitimate target of the submarine was a warship. Under the maritime law of 1907, however, merchantmen could be sunk provided that the U-boat commander had sent a boarding party on board and was certain that the ship was carrying prohibited cargo. Even then the commander was also responsible for the subsequent safety of the ship's crew, and no less a person than Winston Churchill opined that sinking merchant vessels would never be done by a civilised power. However there were 'accidents' with the French ferry *Admiral Ganteaume* sunk in the Channel with 2,500 Belgian refugees on board. By 1915 Britain had established a complete blockade on all German ports and Germany responded with an order that *any* Allied ship would be sunk without warning, including merchant ships. So it was that on 27 March 1915 the merchantman *Vosges*, 1,295 tons, Bordeaux to Liverpool with general cargo, became the first casualty in Cornish waters. She was attacked by *U-28* 23 miles W by N off Trevose and, after the crew had taken to their lifeboats, sunk by gunfire.

The *Drumcree*, a larger vessel of 4,052 tons, sailing in ballast from Barry to Port Arthur with a crew of thirty-six, was 11 miles north-east of Trevose in hazy weather on 18 May, when the third officer saw the track of a torpedo at 100 yards distance. The ship was hit amidships, destroying the radar and injuring the operator so no distress signals could be sent. Capt. Hodgson ordered the boats to be lowered. The SS *Pontos* was in the vicinity and was asked to take the *Drumcree* in tow, but shortly after 3.35p.m. a second torpedo struck aft and she began to sink. The crew took to the boats and the SS *Pontos* cut the tow line and picked up the crew. The U-boat's periscope was visible but she did not interfere. At 5.30 the *Drumcree* sank by the bow and the SS *Pontos*, fearing for her own survival, made for Cardiff at full speed where she landed the survivors.

Following the torpedoing of the collier *Dumfries* on 19 May, the next to be attacked was the *Armenian*, Newport to Avonmouth, 5,755 tons, carrying some 1,420 mules destined for the armies in France. She was 20 miles west of Trevose when the U-boat (*U-38*) was first sighted on the surface at 6.40p.m. on 28 June. Capt. Irickey first tried to ram the U-boat but then ran for Trevose. The U-boat soon overhauled the *Armenian* and began to shell her. After thirty minutes she was so badly damaged that she had to stop engines and the crew took to the boats. As soon as they were clear the U-boat sank her with two torpedoes, the *Armenian* sinking almost vertically by the bow. One of the lifeboats capsized as it was being lowered into the water and the survivors spent a miserable twelve hours in the boats and rafts before being picked up by the Belgian trawler *President Stevens* which landed them at Avonmouth. Of her crew, nine were killed, as were twenty cattle attendants. Another fourteen were wounded. Of the poor mules there was no mention. The Navy's response was to intensify coastal patrols to keep the U-boats submerged. Patrol Area XIV, stretching from Hartland Point round Land's End to Looe, saw a build-up of surveillance vessels, eventually comprising two armed steam yachts, fifty-five armed trawlers, fourteen motor launches and forty-four steam drifters armed with 3-pounder guns.

However in the early days the U-boat attacks continued almost unopposed. The colliers *Magda* and *Sverresborg* were both torpedoed and sunk by *U-27* on 18 August, 8 miles north of Trevose. But on the next day, as a triumphant *U-27* was closing in to finish off the SS *Nicosian*, 37 miles west of Bishop Rock, her captain paid little attention to a rusty-looking tramp steamer flying the US flag. The steamer came to within 600 yards of the U-boat and then – transformation. The covers were taken off, revealing twelve 12-pounder guns; the Stars and Stripes were replaced by the White Ensign, and all hell broke loose. *U-27* was facing the most successful 'Q-ship' *Barralong*, an armed anti-submarine vessel mocked up to look like a sitting duck. She shelled the U-boat and recorded thirty-four hits on her. As the U-boat sank, Capt. Wenger and twelve of the crew swam towards the *Nicosian* and tried to climb aboard by the ladders. The *Baralong's* marksmen picked off eight of them and a party of Royal Marines went across by boat and 'finished the job'. Revenge was undoubtedly sweet.

The sinking of the liner *Lusitania* on 7 May with the loss of 1,198 lives had caused massive outrage in both America and Britain and *'Remember the Lusitania'* was a watchword of the 'Q-ships'. Rioting mobs in Liverpool and London sacked shops with Germanic names and the Government ordered the arrest of up to 30,000 'alien' males. To keep America out of the war the Kaiser imposed severe restrictions on attacking large passenger vessels and on 18 September called off unrestricted U-boat warfare completely. (In all fairness, it must be stated that the Kaiser was always opposed to the indiscriminate use of the U-boat, having stated: 'Gentlemen, always realise that our sword must be clean. We are not waging war against women and children. We wish to fight this war as gentlemen!' Unfortunately, his chief adviser, Admiral von Pohl, just wanted victory on any terms.)

The German tactics were now to attempt to negotiate a peace with the proviso that if they were unsuccessful the U-boats could be let loose again and the lack of cooperation from the Allies would be to blame. The German position was strengthened by the fact that the success of the Q-ship *Barralong* was described as 'cold-blooded murder' by the neutral American press. The negotiations went nowhere and the U-boat blockade resumed. Torpedoes were expensive – especially if they missed the target – and for smaller vessels the U-boat tactic was to surface near the vessel, order the crew to leave and then place scuttling charges on board and sink her. The Padstow fishing smacks *ELG* and *T&AC*, both of 25 tons, were sunk in this fashion some 20 miles NW of Trevose on 1 December 1916.

After the *Lusitania's* sinking, the Admiralty felt, or rather hoped, that the war against the U-boat could be further supported from the air. Discussions concerning the use of aircraft

Left: The loss of another merchantman. (Hurd)

Below: Death dealers: four forward torpedo tubes on a submarine. (W.C.)

Arming the merchantmen; a deck gun is winched aboard a trawler. (Hurd)

Armed and ready. (Hurd)

against the U-boat began back in 1911, but at that time the unreliability of the internal combustion engine was a drawback (it must be remembered that Louis Bleriot took a cash prize of £4,000 for the feat of first crossing the Channel by air only in 1909). However the use of airplanes, seaplanes and airships was seen to be an ideal deterrent against the U-boat, not to sink them outright – that would be a bonus – but to keep them submerged. At the time the submarine was considered chiefly as an armed boat which could submerge rather than the underwater killer of the Second World War. Indeed the submarine looked very much like a surface craft in its early design. So if the U-boat was forced to dive, it could not carry out its blockade duties and our vital supplies could get through.

In the summer of 1914 the Navy had fifty-two seaplanes and seven non-rigid airships. The airships soon became nicknamed 'blimps', so called because this was the echoing sound made when the gas bag was flicked with a finger. The standard airship, SS (Submarine Scout) had a 60,000cu.ft gas bag, a BE2 aeroplane fuselage and a 70hp Renault motor. It flew at fifty knots for eight hours and had a crew of two with a bomb load of 160lb. By 1915 there were twenty-nine in service. A network of airships based at strategic points around the British Isles would be able to act as U-boat spotters and could be adapted to carry bombs. (The excellent account *U-boat Hunters: Cornwall's Air War 1916–19* by Peter London (Truran) tells the full story.) Sometimes the airship was

A merchant seaman's gun crew. (Hurd)

able to lay a bomb pattern in the U-boat track and make a kill, but on other occasions the U-boat stayed surfaced and used its deck gun to shoot the airship down, as happened to airship *C23a*, shot down in Crantock Bay off Newquay on 10 May 1918.

Cornwall's main airship base was at the Mullion, set up in March 1916, but our interest in Trevose Head will focus on the airstrip at Padstow/Crugmeer which came into being in May 1918, following the shift of U-boat activity away from the high seas, where they had been thwarted by the convoy system, and into coastal waters. Sixty per cent of shipping losses in the latter quarter of 1917 were recorded within 10 miles of the coast and the coasts of Cornwall and Devon were regarded as the most dangerous. The site chosen was a fifty-acre field at Crugmeer with a run of 1,500ft across the cliff top. It was to accommodate DH6 two-seater biplanes, but also had a mast at which visiting airships could moor. The original name was going to be 'Trevose Head' but being 5 miles distant this idea was dropped.

Peter London is not very complimentary to the DH6s, Padstow's first intake: 'It was a languid performer … a maximum bomb load of 100lb was possible – provided the pilot flew alone … accidents involving the Padstow DH6s were numerous …' One ran out of fuel and landed in the sea but was towed back to Padstow by a passing vessel where (a nice touch) it was dried out and re-entered service. The fact the DH6 floated well after ditching was considered a plus. Another struck a second plane on landing and went over the cliff into the sea, its crew of two surviving miraculously.

However there was some action against the fiendish Hun. On 23 July 1918, Capt. Goodfellow of Padstow's 250 Squadron dropped a bomb on a U-boat 3 miles off

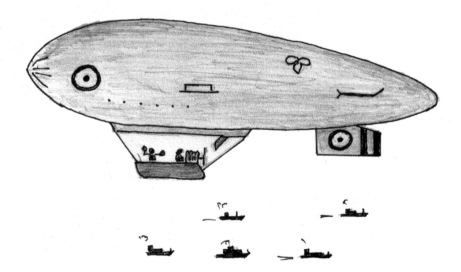

An 'SS Scout' on patrol over a convoy off the Cornish coast, signalling by semaphore. (Drawn from Peter London, 1999)

Lookout for U-boats. (Hurd)

A superb photograph of a convoy in 1916. (Hurd)

The remains of Crugmeer aerodrome and quarters.

The much-derided DH6: Cornwall's first U-boat hunter. (Drawn from Peter London, 1999)

Crugmeer 'landing strip' with Gulland Island ahead.

Trevose, and on 27 July Lt Tremellion attacked a U-boat with a 65lb bomb. Neither of these attacks produced a clear kill. But on 13 August Lt Shorter in *C5075* spotted a surfaced U-boat off Newquay and dropped two small bombs in the U-boat's track as it dived. Maddeningly they failed to explode. London adds ironically, 'Ten days later, as if exhausted by its effort, *C5075* force-landed in the sea.' However the sixty-nine DH6s which patrolled from Crugmeer and the Mullion did have a deterrent effect. The U-boat captains could never be sure whether the approaching plane was armed or not and so diving was the standard response. Their successor, the DH9, was a better aircraft and was able to attack the U-boats in earnest. The Padstow station closed in March 1919. The station's airship mooring mast was purchased for scrap by Richard Parkyn Snr, landlord of the at St Merryn crossroads where, in the Cornish fashion, it was left on the roadside verge for many years.

By 1917 unrestricted U-boat warfare was resumed. Argus of the *West Briton* stated on 5 February 1917: 'We have reached a new phase of the Great War. The Germans have resolved to stake everything on the chance of starving us to exhaustion. This is what their sink-on-sight policy is all about.' And he was spot on. Between February and April 1917 the massacre of merchant shipping began: February 520,000 tons; March 564,000 tons; April 860,000 tons. The 'Western Approaches' became the graveyard of British shipping. Danger to merchant ships was exacerbated by the Allies' increasing use of 'Q-ships', as we have already seen. This gave the U-boat captains a problem. They did not know which merchantmen were armed, but if they stayed submerged and used torpedoes then their effectiveness was limited to a small and expensive payload. On 30 January 1917 an unnamed U-boat sunk eight fishing vessels in an area roughly 30 miles NW of Trevose. The smacks *Euonymous, Helena Samuel, Marcell C, Merit, Trevone, WAH* and *Wetherill* were all sunk by gunfire. This 'feat' of seamanship was repeated on 12 March when eight more fishing vessels were captured and scuttled about 10 miles NNW of Trevose: *CAS, Ena, Gracia, Hyacynth, Inter-Nos, Jessamine, Proverb* and *Rivina* were all lost. Thankfully the U-boat skipper allowed the crews to leave in their boats on each occasion.

It must be added that during this period the 'natural inclination' of the Cornishman to make good use of any sea-borne bounty that came shorewards was maintained. The story of one enterprising chap from Constantine Bay has it that he was hired by the coastguard to take a barrel of whisky which had floated ashore up to the coastguard station. This he undertook, stopping only to decant the contents of the barrel into an empty keg and fill the coastguard's barrel with water of an unsavoury consistency. It was duly despatched from Padstow railway station and the thief calmly collected his pay for services rendered.

In April 1917 America, at last, entered the war and the massive American arms industry was put into full production turning out one destroyer in six weeks, compared with Britain's

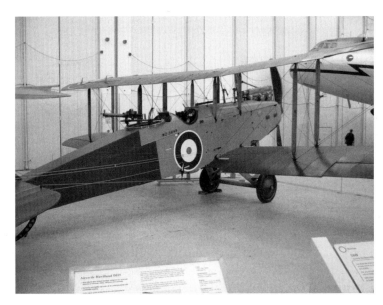

The DH9; a much better replacement for the lumbering DH6. (Alex Layzell, W.C.)

one year and a half. Thus any ship lost to the U-boats could be made good. This was of little comfort to the *Plutus*, 1,189 tons, Rouen to Barry Roads, torpedoed by *UC-47* on 24 April, or the *Warnow*. She was carrying railway components under sealed orders from Penarth when she was torpedoed by *UC-48* at 3a.m. on 2 May 1917. The ship sank very quickly and the captain and thirteen crew died immediately. The chief officer and five crew were left clinging to an upturned lifeboat. The U-boat surfaced and came alongside the struggling men. 'Give me your ship's name and cargo,' commanded the captain. The men refused. 'Help us get this boat right way up,' pleaded the men. The request was denied and the U-boat made off. The men were in the water for over two and a half hours before being picked up by the French vessel SS *Duguesclin* and landed at Penzance.

Worse was to befall the crew of the brigantine *Jane Williamson*, Liverpool to Cherbourg, with coal. She was attacked by a surfaced U-boat 20 miles off Trevose on 10 September 1917 at 4p.m. The crew left the sinking vessel in their lifeboat, no doubt hoping that the U-boat captain would be satisfied with his 'prize'. The German, however, began to fire on the lifeboat, killing the captain and three crew. The survivors were picked up by a trawler and landed at Penzance. The captain destroyed the ship's papers before the vessel sank.

The crew of the *Townley*, 2,476 tons, Devonport to Barry Roads in ballast, must have thought themselves fortunate when all twenty-four of them got away from their vessel which was torpedoed by *U-46* on 31 January 1918. The ship sank at 9.30p.m. At 11p.m. the chief officer sighted a topsail schooner which came within a few yards of the men but then to their dismay turned away. At midnight a steamship was sighted and signalled to but she maintained her course. At daylight, land was seen some 12 miles off. At 9p.m. that evening the Belgian trawler *Ibis IV* hove into view and closed in on their lifeboat. Then disaster; as the men were endeavouring to board her (at about midnight) the boat capsized and the captain, the chief engineer and three crew were drowned.

By 1918 the German position was becoming desperate. The war was slowly being lost. At sea the convoy system of the Allies, although initially resisted by both the naval

The hospital ship *Glenart Castle* torpedoed without warning on 25 February 1918.

Hartland Point lighthouse, where a plaque was placed to remember those lost on the *Glenart Castle*.

establishment and the merchant marine, had thwarted the U-boat to such an extent that any British vessel sunk was deemed a success. As a consequence, hospital ships, passenger vessels requisitioned by the Navy, were sitting ducks for the frustrated U-boat captains. They were painted white with highly visible illuminated red crosses and had a green band painted all round the vessel. At night they carried full navigation and deck lights to make them visible. On 4 January 1918 HMHS *Rewa*, 7,305 tons, was completing its long voyage from Greece to Cardiff via Malta carrying 560 people in all, including thirty cot cases and walking wounded, many suffering from malaria. She was intercepted by *U-55*, under Kapt. Wilhelm Werner, at a position given variously as 33 miles north of Newquay or 19 miles west by a half west of Hartland Point and torpedoed. By a miracle only four lives were lost. Under the calm directions of Capt. Drake, fourteen lifeboats were launched while the *Rewa* slowly sank by the head. The flotilla of lifeboats was picked up by two trawlers and the tanker *Paul Paix* some four hours later.

This luck did not last, however. On 25 February 1918, HMHS *Glenart Castle*, 6,824 tons, left Newport bound for Brest to take on patients. She carried 186 persons, comprising 122 crew, and about fifty medical staff. At 4a.m. on 26 February she was hit by a torpedo abaft of the engine room fired by *UC-56*. The captain, Lt-Com. Burt, who lost his life in the sinking, rang the engine room to stop engines and gave six blasts on the ship's siren to abandon ship. The vessel went down quickly, within seven minutes, and sank before all the lifeboats could be made ready. John Hill, second mate on the *Swansea Castle*, saw the brightly lit hospital ship crossing their bows in the distance ahead and then – total darkness. He thought he saw something which 'looked like Noah's Ark' on their beam but quickly realised it was the U-boat which slipped away in the night.

Tom Matthews, bosun's mate, reckoned that seven lifeboats got away with people on board and two empty ones floated off the poop. His boat, containing twenty-two survivors, was the only boat to make it, being picked up by a French yawl, *Feon*, 6 miles off Lundy and then landed at Swansea. Alfred Bale, thrown into the water when the vessel sank, came up and swam to an upturned boat with three crew clinging on to its side. They thought that help was at hand when they saw a schooner coming towards them but this turned out to be the U-boat overseeing its work. As Bale said: 'We'll get nothing out of him.' Of the 186 people on board only thirty-one survived, twenty-two in the lifeboat and nine others who were pulled from the water by the crew men of USS *Parker* who, despite the temperature of the water and the heavy seas, jumped in and swam to the raft. A monument to those who died was erected on Hartland Point on 26 February 2002.

In an almost identical location to the *Glenart Castle*, HMHS *Guildford Castle*, with 438 patients on board, was torpedoed on 10 March 1918. Miraculously the torpedo which struck the ship full on the port side failed to detonate. On examination in port, the torpedo had apparently bounced off the vessel and slewed down the ship's side where it was struck by one of the ship's propellers.

This poster reflects the mood of the time after the sinking of the hospital ships. (W.C.)

On 3 September 1918, *UB-125* was waiting submerged 4 miles NW of Trevose when two merchant ships were sighted, the *Lake Owens*, a US vessel, 2,308 tons, Nantes to Barry Roads in ballast, and the *Brava* of Lisbon, 3,184 tons, Bordeaux to Cardiff with pit props. Both vessels were torpedoed and sunk in quick succession. Happily both crews got away in their own boats and forty-four survivors from both vessels landed at Newquay with Capt. Rocha of the *Brava* and thirty crew making it to Padstow. *UB-117* accounted for the *Acadian*, a Canadian ore carrier of 2,305 tons. She was on her long voyage from Bilbao to Ayr when she was torpedoed amidships on 16 September 1918 11 miles south-west of Trevose. Twenty-four crew were lost including the captain and one passenger who was a stowaway. The sole survivor said he saw the track of the torpedo and that the ship sank in two minutes with the fore and aft masts touching as she went down. He managed to get on a raft and was picked up at 9a.m. the following day by HMS *Wyre* and landed at Falmouth.

The Wireless Telegraph Operator on the *Lavernock*, 2,406 tons Bilbao to Glasgow with iron ore, climbed into his bunk at midnight on 17 September 1918. The next thing he knew, he found himself in the sea 300 yards from his sinking ship. The only other survivor of the crew of twenty-eight was the lookout on the port side who said that, after the explosion, he was taken deep down into the sea by the suction of the sinking ship, but surfaced and managed to swim to a boat which had stayed afloat. He was picked up by SS *Wild Rose* and taken to St Ives. The Wireless Telegraph Operator clung to wreckage from the cabin for twelve hours before being rescued by an armed trawler and taken to Falmouth. The enemy U-boat was again *UB-117* which also had the dubious distinction of sinking the last vessel in these waters. The next day, 18 September 1918, the *John O. Scott* was torpedoed 9 miles W by N of Trevose. Eighteen of her crew were lost. The sole survivor, a Greek seaman, clung to wreckage for nine and a half hours and was picked up by a motor launch and landed at Newquay.

By the end of the 'Great War', the U-boats had sunk over 5,000 British ships totalling 9 million tons. This, out of a total British merchant shipping fleet of 21 million tons, shows quite how important the victory at sea was to the survival of Britain. The majority of the U-boats were surrendered to the British at Harwich. It may be of some comfort to learn that five of the 'marauders of Trevose' were destroyed in action. *U-28* foundered off the North Cape, holed by the debris from the SS *Olive Branch*, a munitions ship which she had just torpedoed on 2 September 1918; *UC-48* was badly damaged by HMS *Loyal* in the Channel and limped to Ferrol (Spain) on 23 March 1918; *UB-109* was sunk by a mine in the Dover Straits on 19 August 1918.; *U-27* was destroyed off the Scillies by gunfire from the Q-ship *Barralong* and *UC-51* was mined off Start Point on 17 November 1918.

1 ELIZABETH ELEANOR 1917	28 DUMFRIES 1915	55 RUNSWICK 1918
2 COTTINGHAM 1915	29 GIRDLENESS 1918	56 ESMERELDA 1918
3 NORTHFIELD 1918	30 WISBECH 1917	57 POTRUGAL 1918
4 ADA 1917	31 VOSGES 1915	58 JOHN O'SCOTT 1918
5 ELG 1916	32 CAS 1917	59 JANE WILLIAMSON 1917
6 T&AC 1916	33 ENA 1917	60 ANNA SOPHIE 1918
7 EUONYMOUS 1917	34 PLUTUS 1917	61 POLDOWN 1917
8 H.S. GLENART CASTLE 1918	35 DRUMCHREE 1915	62 BRISSONS 1917
9 ANNIE B. SMITH 1918	36 HOLKAR 1918	63 MINISTRE BERNACRT 1915
10 TREVONE 1917	37 ESSONITE 1917	64 PRESIDENT 1917
11 WAH 1917	38 PIERRE 1917	65 THRIFT 1917
12 WETHERILL 1917	39 MAGDA 1915	66 WARNOW 1917
13 1918 H.S. REWA	40 SVERRESBORG 1915	67 CARL 1917
14 ST CROIX 1917	41 ROSSENDALE 1918	68 SAIMA 1918
15 MERIT 1917	42 MADRYN 1919	69 TAGONA 1918
16 TOWNELEY 1918	43 KINDLY LIGHT 1918	70 ARMENIAN 1915
17 PROVERB 1917	44 HUNSGROVE 1918	71 CASSARA 1918
18 HYACINTH 1917	45 BRISE 1918	72 LAVERNOCK 1918
19 INVERLYON 1917	46 STAR OF FREEDOM 1917	73 ONEGA 1918
20 RIVINIA 1917	47 CAVALLO 1918	74 METFJORD 1918
21 INTERNOS 1917	48 ST JOSEPH 1918	75 ORFORDNESS 1918
22 MARCELL C 1917	49 ST GEORGES 1918	76 ALTAIR 1917
23 LENTLILY 1917	50 INGRID II 1917	77 LAKE EDON 1918
24 BRISK 1918	51 STANSBERT 1916	78 PETERSHAM 1918
25 DILIGENT 1917	52 BRAVA 1918	79 ARCADIAN 1918
26 NELLIE 1917	53 SAPHIR 1918	80 CHRISTINA 1918
27 GRACIA 1917	54 LAKE OWENS 1918	81 HELENA SAMUEL 1917

40

05.40W
50.60N

50.50N

50.40N

50.30N

50.20N

Waiting for rescue: A common experience for merchant seamen in the U-boat war. (Hurd)

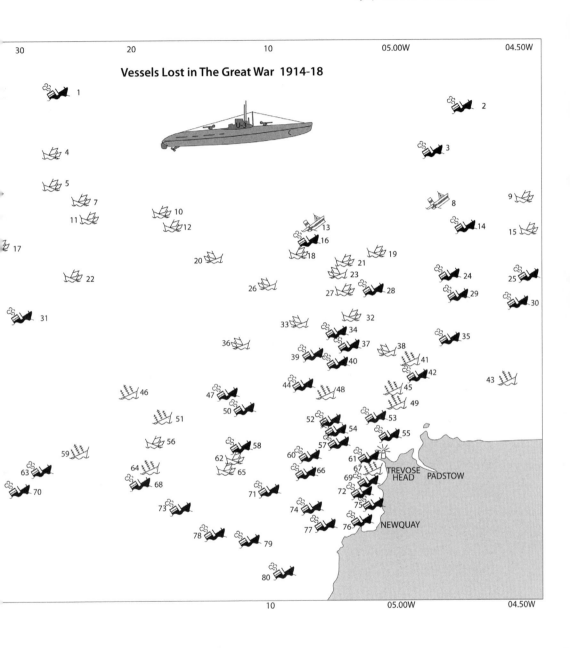

Vessels Lost in The Great War 1914-18

TREVOSE HEAD · PADSTOW

NEWQUAY

Fore-Aft rigger   Square rigger   Steam   Hospital ship

CHAPTER 4

SHIP LOSSES 1918 TO THE PRESENT

The period from the end of the First World War to the present is noted for fewer vessels lost off north Cornwall, including the spectacular losses of HMCS *Regina* and HMS *Warwick* in the Second World War. Up to the present there have only been twenty-one losses, seven of which were war casualties (1940–45). Improved sea-worthiness of ships, improved navigation and improved monitoring by wireless and satellite have drastically cut the chances of a sailor's life being all too short. Of course, the fall in coastal trade and the overall decline in British shipping have greatly reduced the number of vessels passing Trevose Head. At present an ocean-going vessel passing Trevose Head is a rare sight indeed.

Nonetheless those time-honoured hazards – leaky vessels, collision and the ever-dangerous sea fog – still accounted for some unfortunate ships. The *Emily*, June 1919, the *Bratto*, November 1920, and the *Voluntaire*, March 1924, all foundered after developing major leaks. All crews were happily saved. The SS *White Rose*, 2,691 tons, Boulogne to Llanelli, sank after colliding with the SS *Fantee* on 20 March 1919. The *Claretta*, a collier of 500 tons from Cardiff to Granville, collided with SS *Borderland* 3 miles west of Trevose in dense fog and sank on 31 August 1930. In the same fog bank, slightly further westward, the collier *Shoreham*, 805 tons, Swansea to Rouen, ran into the SS *Annik* and sank. The SS *Annik* picked up the crew from the water. On New Year's Day 1938, the schooner *Sylvabelle*, with pit props from Trinite-sur-Mer to Cardiff, collided with the SS *Ilse* and was abandoned. In all these accidents the crews were saved. Two men of a crew of twenty were lost, however, when the *Kai*, a collier of 1,251 tons, Swansea to Southampton, struck submerged wreckage and foundered on 1 February 1941. Ten men were picked up by the St Ives lifeboat and eight by the SS *Ilesman*.

THE SECOND WORLD WAR

It was not recorded whether the 'sunken wreckage' was a casualty of war, but the first noted war casualty in these waters was the SS *Empire Otter*, 4,670 tons, with crude oil from Southampton to Avonmouth. She blew up when she struck a mine 10 miles NE of

A jaunty postcard to keep the nation's spirits up.

Priming depth charges aboard a destroyer; note the obligatory 'ciggy'. (Hurd)

Got the blighter! Destruction of a U-boat by depth charge. (Hurd)

Trevose. Ironically it was thought to be a British mine. The fate of the crew is unknown. In the early phase of the war, air attacks by Luftwaffe planes were an additional hazard and the *Tregor*, a motor vessel carrying flour from Avonmouth to Hale, was strafed and abandoned by its crew of six on 4 May 1941. The vessel was later on tow to Padstow when it sank. A similar fate befell the *Viva II*, a motorised yacht requisitioned by the Navy as an anti-submarine vessel. She was attacked and sank on 8 May.

Unlike the maritime situation in the Great War, the waters off Trevose Head were relatively free of major U-boat activity, especially in the opening years of the Second World War. The Navy and the Merchant Marine adopted the convoy system from the beginning to thwart the 'wolf-packs', while the increasing development of depth charges and the RAF's ability to strike from the air kept the U-boat at bay, i.e. submerged. It was only later when the German plan changed to attacking ships in coastal waters that tragedies occurred.

THE SINKING OF THE *WARWICK*

Our position was some twelve to fourteen miles from Trevose Head. The crew were on deck, gutting and washing the catch ready for stowing them down the fish hold in ice. Glancing ahead I could see the destroyers had turned and were coming toward us. They would pass some two or three miles on our starboard side … the nearest (destroyer) was stemming us. I immediately went to the flag locker, where our flag signals denoting our ship's name were always bent on the halyards to hoist on the approach of one of our ships … Noticing the destroyer turning on to her original course I picked up the ship's binoculars and focussed them on the ship. The destroyer was now in bold relief. Then it happened. The time was 11.55a.m. There was a cloud of smoke tinted with flame and a tremendous explosion from her stern. She was before the wind causing smoke to envelop her for a moment. This cleared and the ship was nosing her way through the water. At this time she seemed all right. Then a second explosion came just aft of her funnel. The aft part of the ship rolled over to starboard and sank beneath the waves. Hardly anyone could have got clear from that part of the ship. The suddenness of the two torpedoes could not have given them a chance. I was dumbstruck.

This was how, on 20 February 1944, Victor Crisp, skipper of the trawler *Lady Luck* of Padstow, witnessed the sinking of the destroyer HMS *Warwick* by *U-413*.

The *Warwick*, a now-ageing Second World War vessel, flagship of Admiral Keyes in 1918, and HMS *Scimitar* had been sent from Devonport after it was reported that a U-boat had been picked up off the north Cornwall coast in the path of a convoy bound for Liverpool. Both vessels had been searching for U-boats by ASDIC but, as recorded much later by Capt. Poel, the U-boat's skipper kept his vessel head on to the *Warwick* to give a smaller silhouette and was helped by the currents off Trevose which distorted the ASDIC echoes. Only one torpedo struck the *Warwick*; the major damage, according to Poel, was caused by the blowing up of the boiler. *U-413* had been under Trevose Head for several days,

'The *Lady Luck*': the painting by Padstow artist Derek Lindsay of *Lady Luck* steaming to help survivors from HMS *Warwick*. (Padstow Museum)

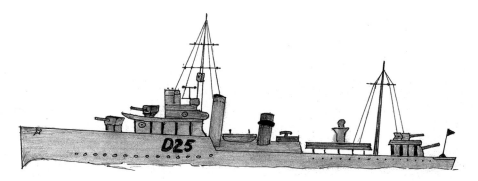

HMS *Warwick* torpedoed and sunk on 20 February 1944. A loss much mourned by the Padstow community.

surfacing at night to charge batteries and freshen up the air in the sub. Poel was aware of two destroyers in the area (HMS *Warwick* and HMS *Scimitar*) and after the sinking of the *Warwick*, the *Scimitar* attempted to depth charge *U-413* but the U-boat managed to escape and kept submerged for the next four days. Karl Hutterer, chief engineer on *U-413*, said he heard the call signs of three destroyers. The third destroyer was HMS *Wensleydale*, also a witness to the disaster.

HMS *Wensleydale* was on convoy escort duty with two armed trawlers steaming towards Lundy. Lt-Com. H. Lehmann, PO on the *Wensleydale*, recalls:

A W Class destroyer was steaming towards us on an opposite course … we passed each other about 100 yards distance and waved to each other. When we were about 500 yards apart I saw a small mushroom of smoke on the starboard quarter of the W Class destroyer and then in seconds heard a muffled explosion; the stern broke off and immediately passed down the side of the stricken ship as she slowed down and began to settle by the stern; the props were still turning in the air; men began to dive overboard. The klaxon sounded 'Action Stations' and as I turned to run down the starboard side of the deck I saw, out of the corner of my eye, an indistinct track of something coming at our stern. The track missed our stern by about 10 yards. We made contact with a U-boat and dropped depth charges to no avail. Our orders were to stay with the convoy and not stop for survivors. I can still see the men in the sea as we steamed through them. Just like the story by Monsarrat in 'the Cruel Sea'.

One of those unfortunates was telegraphist K.G. Holmes who had escaped from the sinking ship only to find himself entangled in a wire rope and struggling with another rating who had no lifebelt. They were both sucked down with the undertow. When he surfaced, alone, he was delighted to see the *Wensleydale* steaming towards him, then steaming past him, and to make matters worse dropping depth charges along the way.

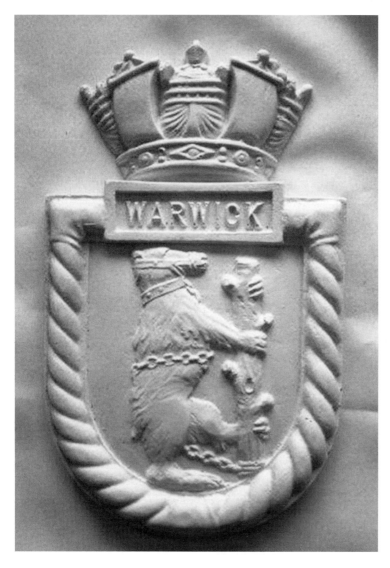

The crest of HMS *Warwick*; she was the first vessel to be badged. (Puddicombe)

Ernie Moseley, a Birmingham lad of nineteen, was a rating on the *Wensleydale*. He was told to take a tot of rum up to L/S Coalville in the director tower.

As I said, 'Here's your tot', there was this almighty explosion on the starboard quarter and this ship went up in the air. 'Action Stations' went – and the tot went in the air too! I ran for my tin hat and collided with another bloke coming from the forward mess deck as I was going in. I got to my station and said, 'What's up, Jock?' He said, 'It's the *Warwick*.' Anyway we settled down later and Coalville got up and said, 'Where's my tot?' All heads turned to me. 'I dropped it.' 'You what?' he roared. 'Whatever you do don't let him get hold of my tot again!'

By 11.47a.m. the *Warwick* had gone, three minutes after the torpedo struck. The survivors were now swimming for their lives in a sea of thick black oil from the shattered fuel tanks. HMS *Scimitar* came in to the rescue and the Fleet Air Arm dropped self-inflating liferafts. The Belgian fishing boat *Chrisopher Columbus* came to help, her crew jumping into the water to assist the cold and weary sailors. Pride of place in the list of rescuers must go to local Padstow fisherman Vic Crisp of the *Lady Luck* who, having witnessed the incident, now went into rescue mode:

> As we approached the sailors in the water, our small boat was made ready for launching. At the time my ship was short-handed and as three of my crew were over sixty years of age, I decided against launching. Our own vessel was low in the water so we could reach over the side and pull the survivors on board. The oil fuel from the destroyer was covering the area. Men were calling for help. I decided to pick up first the men who were in the water. As we began to pull the men on board I saw the terrible mess with which they were covered – thick sticky oil.

Crisp and his crew succeeded in getting the men out of the water and down into the cabin to get some warmth into their bodies. He then had to steer the *Lady Luck* to the rafts. One man, who seemed in a pretty bad state, was proving impossible to haul aboard until Crisp noticed that his legs were caught in the hand line running round the raft. Having cut that they were able to rescue him. Next, they made for a larger raft with eleven men on board. They threw a line over, and one of the injured men grabbed it. Then they pulled the raft alongside. They carried all eleven off the raft. As these seemed to be the last survivors Crisp ordered full speed for Padstow, but then he noticed another body in the water and it took all four of them to pull him aboard. Crisp now had forty-plus bodies on his ship.

On the journey back to Padstow, *Lady Luck* was met by an Air Sea Rescue Launch which ordered him by hailer that he should transfer the survivors to them. Crisp continued:

The final moments of HMS *Warwick* taken from HMS *Scimitar*. (Puddicombe)

This did not make sense to me. We were flying the W Flag, 'I need a doctor'. With the scanty requirements from my medical box and a knowledge that nothing more could be done, I was concerned with a badly burned sailor and whether he would live. I went to the cabin and spoke with the Warwick's commander. He asked me how his men were and how long before we would be at the quayside. 'As well as can be expected. In another half hour we will be moored at the quay. I am worried about the severely burned man and we will only just make it as the ebb is now running out of the river.'

'Ignore him and carry on,' said the commander.

Once berthed at Padstow the survivors were taken off to St Merryn Airbase, and a welcoming basin full of rum. Crisp, however, was left with 'a little problem'. Because of the U-boat activity the Naval Authorities ordered that no vessel should sail until further notice. *Lady Luck* had an ice store full of fish destined for Milford Haven. Crisp got on the phone to Milford Haven to see what he should do, explaining what had happened. He was told in no uncertain terms that he should have taken the ship and survivors to Milford in the first place:

I replied, 'It's all right for you people, you just sit on your arses and don't realise there's a war on!' With that I hung up the phone.

Normal service was resumed on 24 February, and the next day *Lady Luck* made it to Milford Haven. Far from being given a hero's welcome, Crisp was admonished for not obeying orders and accused of insubordination (bureaucracy as ever rearing its ugly head in the most inappropriate situations). The upshot was that Crisp was asked to 'sign off', i.e. resign:

'Give me the ******* pen!'

Crisp caught the next train back to Padstow. (Unbelievable though it may be, Vic Crisp and *Lady Luck* were never mentioned in dispatches, nor was he called to the subsequent naval inquiry. An 'award' promised to him by the SW Area Fishery Officer never materialised either).

Cdr Rayner's account of the sinking, in his book *Escort*, is a model of professional understatement and naval *sang froid*. After the initial shock of being torpedoed he said:

I looked ahead and saw something floating in the water like a giant metallic whale. Then I could make out our own pennant numbers on it. I was dumbfounded … I ran to the after side of the bridge and looked over … the ship ended just aft of the engine room. What I had seen ahead of us had been my ship's own stern.' 'Abandon ship, Sir?' 'Not bloody likely, No. 1.'

As the ship settled lower in the water:

The deck began to take on an angle … suddenly I was slithering along … I saw Harries, the navigator, going over the side with a polished wooden box in either hand: the chronometer and the sextant. I wished I had someone to laugh with over that one. The sea around me was covered with bobbing heads. 'Come on in Sir. The water's lovely,' they shouted. 'I'm waiting for the Skylark,' I replied. Then I too was swimming.

Rayner was eventually picked up by some men on a Carley float, and despite having been in the vicinity of *Scimitar*'s depth charges while in the water (described as being 'a bit like being punched in the chest, not as bad as I expected'), he was still in command, ordering his men to take turns in being on the float and in the water hanging on to the ropes spliced to the jack stay. He had seen overloaded floats capsize too often.

Harries, the aforementioned carrier of the ship's instruments, survived but his possessions did not. With the increasing cold, he let go of the chronometer first (it would be more expensive to repair). He trod water with the precious sextant until his fingers became numb. Just as he let go of the box he was hauled into a raft but madly tried to dive down for the sextant sinking into the depths. His rescuer promptly knocked him out thinking he 'had gone nuts'.

Of those rescued, six died during the Sunday night. They were buried in the cemetery of St Merryn church – P.O Ford, J.L. Bell, J.C.R. Tower, C.G. Chappel, W.K. Morgan

The graves of the men killed in the *Warwick* disaster in St Merryn church.

Left:Warwick Sunday: a display of *Warwick* memorabilia at the church service at St Merryn.

Opposite: This porthole taken from the *Warwick* wreck site by divers was presented to Padstow Museum by Moira Gill.

Left: The grave of J.L. Bell lost on HMS *Warwick*, 20 February 1944.

and F.S. Young. A remembrance service for the *Warwick* has been held every year since at St Merryn church. Moira Gill, Mayor of St Merryn and churchwarden, was a girl of seven when the *Warwick* went down:

> I had just come out of sunday school in Padstow and my father George, who had just returned home after being torpedoed on the Russian convoys, took me down to the Quay. At first I could see all the trawlers filling up the Quay and the dock area, but as we walked up the Dock there was a sight that I will never forget: men all black with oil, many on stretchers, all waiting to be transported to safety. It is a memory that has stayed with me all these years and to have now met so many of the people involved in that rescue some sixty odd years ago makes our remembrance service more memorable.

The same service also remembers other members of HM Forces killed on that fateful day. At the same time as the *Warwick* and *Scimitar* were hunting *U-413*, a Wellington bomber, HF168, with a crew of six was scrambled from RAF Chivenor to assist the search. She was armed with depth charges, the submariner's nightmare. Contact was abruptly lost with the aircraft and nothing was ever heard of her or her crew again. It was thought that the depth charges must have exploded in the bomb bay when she was out over the sea.

ST. MERRYN CHURCH
SERVICE ROTA FOR FEBRUARY 2010

Sunday 21st February   1st Sunday of Lent
                                      66th Anniversary of the sinking of HMS. Warwick

11.00am.   Holy Communion CW   (S) Alan Baily
                                      (S) Edith Dakin
             Deuteronomy 26: 1-11   (R) Anne Wood
             Romans 10: 8-13   (R) Moira Gill
             Luke 4: 1-13   (R) Canon Julia
                                      (C) Sylvia Copstick
                                      (C) Esther Trenouth

Intercessions: Gerry Chandler

St Merryn church and the Order of Service programme for the annual February service to remember the *Warwick*, held on the nearest Sunday to the date of sinking.

A ship in a bottle model of the *Warwick* in Padstow Museum.

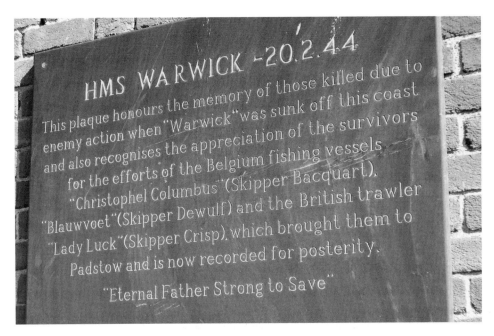

HMS WARWICK -20.2.44

This plaque honours the memory of those killed due to enemy action when "Warwick" was sunk off this coast and also recognises the appreciation of the survivors for the efforts of the Belgium fishing vessels "Christophel Columbus" (Skipper Bacquart), "Blauwvoet" (Skipper Dewulf) and the British trawler "Lady Luck" (Skipper Crisp), which brought them to Padstow and is now recorded for posterity.

"Eternal Father Strong to Save"

The *Warwick* commemorative plaque at Padstow harbour.

Nick Hewitt in his book *Coastal Convoys* provides us with this postscript:

For HMS *Wensleydale*, the wheel turned full circle on 20 August 1944 when along with the destroyers *Vidette* and *Forester* she cornered and sank *U-413* the slayer of the *Warwick*. There was only one survivor, Karl Hutterer, the chief engineer.

THE LOSS OF THE *REGINA*: MINED OR TORPEDOED?

Next to the headstones of the crew of the *Warwick* stand two more of the same white marble, those of J.M. Saulnier and J.C.H. Rathbone. These were two of the crew of the Canadian corvette *Regina*. HMCS *Regina* was a Flower Class corvette, assigned to C-I Escort Group in March 1944. Her remit was to escort vessels from the Bristol Channel ports to assembly areas in preparation for Operation Overlord – the second front in France. On 8 August 1944 she was the sole escort of EBC-66 – a convoy of ten vessels in two columns – and was proceeding south-west along the coast of Cornwall, making a broad zig-zag sweep from ahead of the starboard column to the head of the port column. It was a clear fine evening, and at 9.30p.m the convoy was 8 miles off Trevose Head. Suddenly there was an explosion and steam was seen pouring out of the US Liberty ship *Ezra Weston*, the third ship in the starboard column. The *Ezra Weston* was

7,191 tons, carrying 5,800 tons of army supplies and a deck cargo of trucks. The master of the *Ezra Weston* signalled that he had been hit by a mine. The commander of the *Regina*, Jack Radford, considered this a possibility since the *Ezra Weston* was outside the swept channel and no U-boats had been detected in the vicinity. His supposition was to prove a mistaken one and his subsequent action led to a tragedy.

Radford could see the *Ezra Weston* had a broken back and so advised the master to try to beach her at Padstow. *LCT 644*, a tank landing craft, was in the convoy under the command of Sub-Lt L.G. Read and he was detailed to go alongside and take the crew off the now sinking *Ezra Weston*. The operation took an hour but the deck cargo of vehicles could not be offloaded as there was now no power to drive the winches. The merchant ship continued to move slowly ahead and the *Regina* stayed in the vicinity with engines idling. Then the *Ezra Weston* stopped and *LCT 644* put a line aboard attempting to tow her stern first into shallower waters. Then it happened. The *Regina* was 200ft from the LCT when she exploded and sank in seconds. The crew who were watching the towing operation were blown into the water. Thirty of the crew were killed on board or drowned as the ship went down by the stern. The sixty-six survivors plus the four officers who had stayed on board the *Ezra Weston* to assist the towing operation were rescued by the LCT and the trawler *Jacques Morgand*.

Above left: The grave of Canadian seaman J.M. Saulnier of the *Regina* in St Merryn churchyard.

Above right: The crest of HMCS *Regina*. (Canadian Department of National Defence, W.C.)

HMCS Regina

HMCS *Regina* sunk on 8 August 1944. She was thought to have hit a mine but later it was confirmed by German records that she had been torpedoed.

A vintage LCT in Boston Harbour; these LCTs (Landing Craft Tanks) were also known as LSTs (Landing Ship Tanks) or 'Large Sitting Targets'. (US Navy Photos, W.C.)

The *Jeremiah O Brien*, a well-preserved Liberty ship. 2,751 of these transporters were built and became 'The Bridge of Steel' spanning the North Atlantic. (Mike Hofman, W.C.)

As in all naval disasters choking fuel oil added to the plight of the survivors. On the LCT one can only imagine the chaos and heroism, with Surgeon Lt Gould operating under flashlight with a sterilised carving knife and brandy as anaesthetic (Gould was the surgeon on the *Regina*, himself plucked out of the water and in shock minutes before). He successfully performed a leg amputation on Lionel Racker. The survivors were taken to Padstow and transferred to the RNLI *Princess Mary* (Padstow), ex-RNLI *Sir William Hilary* (Dover) and other small boats. The Padstow crew expressed some annoyance that they had not been called out to the rescue.

At the naval inquiry the cause of the sinkings was uppermost in the debate. None of the witnesses could be certain that it was anything other than a mine which sank the *Ezra Weston* and the *Regina*. In all honesty, Radford would not have stopped his ship if there had been any hint of a U-boat or torpedo attack. However one of the crew of the *Regina* was certain it was a torpedo. As the *Ezra Weston* was the third ship in the convoy 'line', how did the other two ships ahead of her manage to pass over the supposed mine? Radford was not formally criticised for leaving his convoy but was considered to have made a grave error by remaining stopped. But hindsight sometimes brings unwelcome knowledge. It was in fact a U-boat, *U-667*, commanded by Carl Heinz Lang, which had sunk both vessels by torpedo. This fact was not known until well after the war when the German records were examined. *U-667* had been fitted with a *schnorkel* allowing air to be drawn in while the vessel was submerged. Ironically, up to that time she had not recorded one successful attack.

MYSTERY U-BOATS

In the final stages of the war three more vessels were destroyed off Trevose Head. They were destroyed in silence, the explosions unheard, their disappearance unnoticed, their men unmourned until the present century. These were U-boats, fitted with the latest *schnorkel* breathing equipment which enabled them to stay underwater for most of their mission. The *schnorkel* was the answer to the U-boat commander's prayers. If periods of enforced exposure on the surface could be reduced or even rendered unnecessary then the Allies' air patrols would lose their advantage and the true submarine would triumph. Such a simple device – an air pipe extended above the surface at periscope depth with a ball cock to close the pipe and prevent water flooding the boat when waves washed over the inlet – could have been introduced much earlier in the war. Thankfully the Germans did not think they needed it.

So *U-400*, *U-1021* and *U-325* were all despatched from their bases in Norway to sail round Scotland and Ireland and harass the Atlantic convoys bringing supplies to the Channel Ports. This was a change in strategy forced on the U-boat packs by the Allies' improved radar, and the cracking of the German 'Enigma' code. Rather than take on convoys in the mid-Atlantic, the *schnorkel* U-boats were ordered to attack along the coast. This strategy was a blow to the Allies; the coasters, weary of the endless vigilance on the high seas, now had

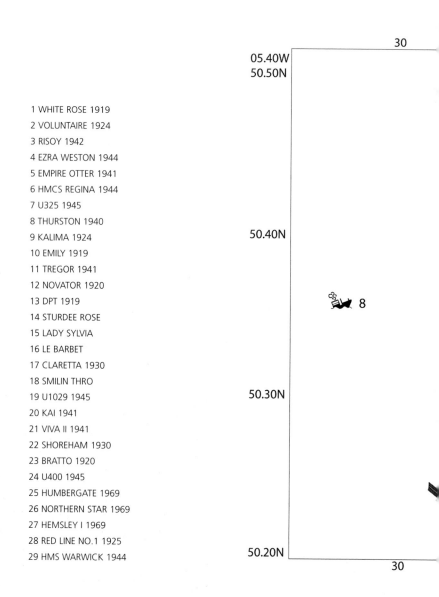

1 WHITE ROSE 1919
2 VOLUNTAIRE 1924
3 RISOY 1942
4 EZRA WESTON 1944
5 EMPIRE OTTER 1941
6 HMCS REGINA 1944
7 U325 1945
8 THURSTON 1940
9 KALIMA 1924
10 EMILY 1919
11 TREGOR 1941
12 NOVATOR 1920
13 DPT 1919
14 STURDEE ROSE
15 LADY SYLVIA
16 LE BARBET
17 CLARETTA 1930
18 SMILIN THRO
19 U1029 1945
20 KAI 1941
21 VIVA II 1941
22 SHOREHAM 1930
23 BRATTO 1920
24 U400 1945
25 HUMBERGATE 1969
26 NORTHERN STAR 1969
27 HEMSLEY I 1969
28 RED LINE NO.1 1925
29 HMS WARWICK 1944

05.40W
50.50N

50.40N

50.30N

50.20N

30

30

8

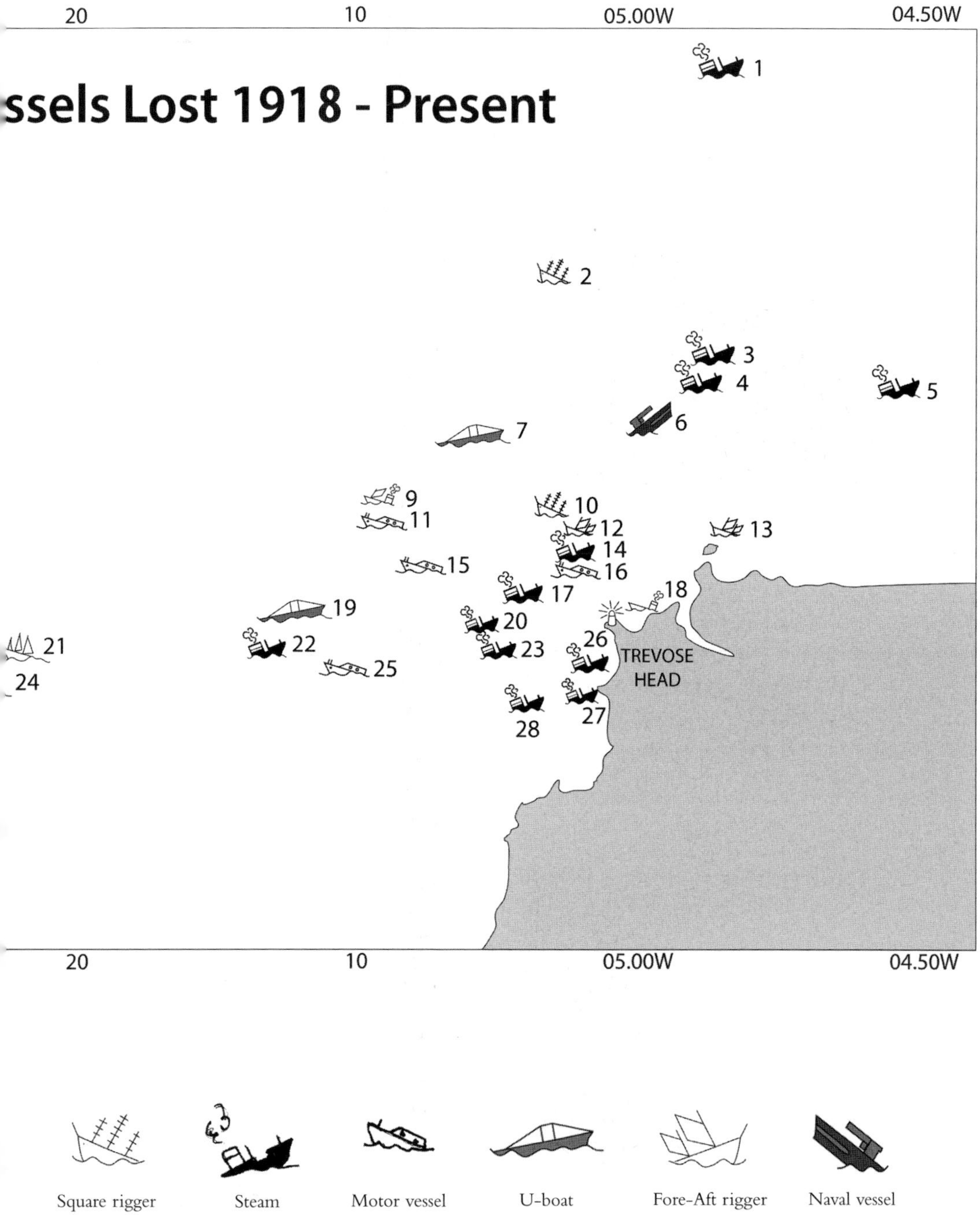

20 10 05.00W 04.50W

ssels Lost 1918 - Present

1

2

3
4

5

6

7

9
11

10
12
14
16

13

15

17

18

19

21

22

24

25

20

23

26

27

28

TREVOSE
HEAD

20 10 05.00W 04.50W

Square rigger   Steam   Motor vessel   U-boat   Fore-Aft rigger   Naval vessel to run the gauntlet again. For the warships, operating off the coast proved tricky as their radar picked up every ship in the vicinity. So which blip was a U-boat and which a small trawler? Fierce battles were fought but the Germans were now losing more U-boats per Allied ship sunk. In desperation the Germans began to deploy small battle units, human torpedoes, miniature subs and explosive motor boats all crewed by eighteen- or nineteen-year-old boys. Fortunately as the Allies, now established in Europe, cut off or cleared German bases the pressure began to ease and surrender was assured.

U-400 was last heard of in December 1944, *U-1021* in March 1945 and *U-325* in April 1945, the last week of the war. *Deep Wreck Mysteries* (Mallinson–Sadler 2006) tells how he and his team came upon these three vessels lying on the sea bed, 60 miles down, off Trevose Head, blown in half by terrible force. Depth charges were mooted as a possibility, but to inflict such catastrophic damage the depth charge would have had to have scored a direct hit on each of the three vessels; an unlikely occurrence. The only explanation possible was that they had been sunk by mines but according to information at hand there were no mines in what was termed the 'Southern Corridor', as the stretch of sea off Trevose Head was kept clear of mines for British convoys and their escorts, which of course the U-boat captains knew only too well.

What these unfortunate captains and their doomed crews did not know – only revealed by British Intelligence after the war – was that a deep mine field had been laid 70ft below the 'Corridor' precisely to destroy U-boats waiting for their prey or diving to escape contact. These mines, each containing up to 500lb of high explosive, accounted for the three U-boats. (It may be a coincidence but the mine which drifted into Padstow on 4 March 1946, which was snared by Messrs Brennan, Brenton and Lindsay and moored in the middle of the river to await the naval disposal squad, could have been one of those selfsame mines from the 'Corridor'.)

The *Hemsley I*. The oldest steamship in the British registry was sailing to the breakers yard in Antwerp. She ran aground in Treyarnon Bay on 12 May 1969. (Padstow Museum)

EPILOGUE

This book is ostensibly a history book, yet looking back it has been a sombre record of death at sea, both in war and peacetime. While the rescue services did what they could there were less stories of success and more of disaster where help was impossible. Hopefully by naming the ships and some of their crew their memory will live on.

I am standing on the sea shore,
A ship sails in the morning breeze and starts for the ocean.
She is an object of beauty and I stand watching her
Till at last she fades on the horizon and someone at my side says:
'She is gone.'

Gone! Where?
Gone from my sight – that is all.
She is just as large in the masts, hull and spars as she was when I saw her
And just as able to bear her load of living freight to its destination.
The diminished size and total loss of sight is in me,
not in her.

And just at the moment when someone at my side says,
'She is gone'
There are others who are watching her coming, and other voices take up a glad shout:
'There she comes'
– and that is dying. An horizon and just the limit of our sight.
Lift us up, Oh Lord, that we may see further.

Bishop Brent
1862 – 1926

BIBLIOGRAPHY

Anderson, E.W., (1973) *Man the Navigator* Priory Press Ltd, London

Bartlett, John, (1996) *Ships of North Cornwall* Tabb House, 7 Church Street, Padstow

Boissier, P., (2003) *Understanding the Rules of the Road* Fernhurst Books, Arundel

Brown, Charles H., (1938) *Nicholls's Seamanship and Nautical Knowledge* (18th Edition) Brown, Son and Ferguson, Glasgow

Carter, Clive, (1970) *Cornish Shipwrecks Vol 2: The North Coast* David & Charles

Chance, T. & Williams, P., (2008) *Lighthouses: The Race to Illuminate the World* New Holland Publishers UK

Cornish Studies Centre, *The Ellis Collection of Newspaper Articles 1750–1992*

Deep Wreck Mysteries, DVD (2006) Mallinson-Sadler Productions; Northern Sky Entertainmen

French, Brian, (2007) *Wrecks and Rescues around Padstow's Doom Bar* Lodenek Press

French, Brian, (2009) *Coastwatch! The NCI Story* History Press, Stroud

Griffiths, M., (1973) *Man the Shipbuilder* Priory Press Ltd, London

Hewitt, Nick, (2008) *Coastal Convoys 1939–45: The Indestructible Highway* Pen and Sword (Maritime)

Hurd, Sir Archibald, (1941) *The Battle of the Seas* Hodder & Stoughton

Jones, Nicollette, (2006) *The Plimsoll Sensation*, Abacus

Lake, Deborah, (2006) *Smoke and Mirrors: Q-ships against U-boats in the First World War* Sutton Publishing Ltd, Stroud

Larn, Richard & Bridget, (1990) *Shipwrecks on Cornwall's North Coast* Tor Mark Press, Redruth

Larn, Richard & Bridget, (1995) *Shipwreck Index of the British Isles – Vol. 1: Scilly, Cornwall, Devon, Dorset* Lloyds Register, London

London, Peter, (2008) *Cornwall's Air War 1916–18* Truran Press

Massie, Robert K., (2007) *Castles of Steel: Britain, Germany and the Winning of the Great War at Sea* Vintage, Random House, London

McGreal, Stephen, (2008) *The War on Hospital Ships 1914–18* Pen & Sword Books Ltd, Barnsley

Nautical Almanac, (2009 edition) Macmillan Reeds

Pearson, Lynn F., (2008) *Lighthouses* Shire Library, Botley, Oxford

Rayner, D.A., (1955) *War at Sea: Escort* Futura

Price, Dr A. (2004) *Aircraft vs Submarine in Two World Wars* Pen and Sword, Yorkshire

Sobel, Dava and Andrews, WJH (1995) *The Ilustrated Longitude* Fourth Estate, London

Spectre, P.H. & Larkin, D. (1991) *Wooden Ship* Houghton Mifflin, USA

Tarrant, Michael (1990) *Cornwall's Lighthouse Heritage* Twelveheads Press, Truro

Thompson, Julian (2005) *The Book of The War at Sea 1914–18* Sidgwick and Jackson

VESSELS LOST 1700–1914

Vessel Name and Voyage	Type of Vessel	Date Lost	Lat/ Long	Location and Cause of Loss	Crew Saved and Lost	Miscellaneous: Registration, Tonnage, Cargo, Captain
Joseph & Elizabeth (London–Bridgewater)	sail	03.02.1741	50.45N 06.00W	Foundered	Crew saved by a London coaster	corn, groceries; Capt. Williams
Margaret (Bristol–Guernsey)	sail	15.09.1752	50.35N 05.00W	Foundered	–	Capt. Bonger
Joseph Ange (Port Vendro–Ruan)	sloop	27.11.1753	50.33N 04.58.50W	Drove ashore due to stress of weather	–	Treguier; Wine; Capt. Pomelee
Carolina (Stockholm–Cork)	sail	17.09.1768	50.34N 05.00W	Foundered	–	Capt. Estander
St George (Dublin–London)	sail	06.12.1768	50.32.05N 05.01.40W	Foundered	–	Capt. Bennett
Elizabeth (London–Dublin)	sail	27.2.1770	50.35N 05.02.06W	Lost main mast W 4m Trevose and drove ashore	One crew lost	Capt. Truman
Three Brothers (Youghal–Portsmouth)	sail	12.03.1775	50.32.40N 04.59.20W	Foundered at St Merryn	–	oats; Capt. Benyon
Nostra Senora Mai des Dios	brigantine	08.04.1782	50.32.40N 05.00W	Stranded in Harlyn Bay	–	Spain; oranges
Catherine and Ann (New York–Cork)	sail	13.05.1795	50.42.40N 04.59.25W	Foundered at St Merryn	–	oats; Capt. Sheffield
Providence (Swansea–?)	sail	13.04.1797	50.46N 05.00W	Foundered	Crew saved in own boat	Falmouth; coal; Capt. Richards

Ship (Route)	Type	Date	Position	Fate	Crew notes	Cargo / Origin / Captain
Mary (Dublin-Kinsale)	sloop	11.05.1797	50.33N 05.05W	Foundered near Padstow	Crew abandoned ship off Ireland	—
St Winnow	sail	29.05.1807	—	Foundered off N Cornwall	—	—
Integrity (Quiberon-?)	sail	21.11.1808	50.32.05N 05.01.40W	Foundered	Crew rescued by cutter *Speedwell*	North Shields; Capt. Cornforth
Elizabeth (Waterford-Shoreham)	sloop	21.11.1808	50.34.05N 05.02.33W	Foundered in Treyarnon Bay	Crew of 2 lost	bacon, butter; Capt. Gill
Two Brothers Cardiff-Portsmouth	sail	24.04.1811	50.38N 05.00W	Foundered	Crew got to Padstow in ship's boat	Capt. Squires
Star (Oporto-Cork)	brig	11.11.1811	50.32.40N 05.00W	Abandoned off Harlyn Bay	Crew all drowned when ship's boat capsized	Dundee; 96Tns; lemons, salt; Capt. Chisholm
Ann	sail	08.11.1814	—	Lost off Trevose Head	—	—
Aimiable Anna (Ribadeo-London)	brigantine	01.03.1815	50.34.05N 04.56.33W	Foundered	—	Spain; nuts, wood, gunstocks; Capt. Santa Marino
Betsey (Portreath-Wales)	brig	15.03.1815	50.35N 05.00W	Sank after leaking	Crew, except boy, got off. Drifted in ship's boat which capsized in Constantine Bay. 3 drowned	copper ore; Capt. Hancock (only survivor)
Concord (Portreath-Wales)	brig	21.04.1815	50.35.00N 05.00W	Foundered	—	Swansea; Capt. Buse
Dolphin (Milford-Porthilly)	sloop	24.04.1815	50.35N 05.00W	Foundered	—	Pwllheli; Capt. Williams
Fortune (Marazion-Swansea)	brig	04.02.1817	50.52.10N 05.00W	Foundered	—	copper ore; Capt. Williams
London (Newport-London)	sail	09.02.1820	50.40N 05.00W	Foundered	Crew reached Padstow in own boat	Plymouth; iron; Capt. Jobscott

Ship (route)	Rig	Date	Position	Circumstance	Notes	Details
Concord (Waterford–Cork)	sail	28.12.1821	50.28.45N 05.00W	Sank in one hour off St Eval	Lost 2 of 5 crew plus 3 passengers, Captain's wife, child & niece	Capt. Hares
Avon (Neath–Dartmouth)	schooner	28.04.1823	50.32N 05.10W	Foundered after leaking	Crew of 4 got off in boat. Picked up by schooner Richmond	Dartmouth; culm; Capt. Tucker
Francis (Newport–Wexford)	brig	01.11.1823	50.32.05N 05.01.40W	Foundered Constantine Bay	–	Newport; 81 Tns; Capt. Williams
L'Amelie (Swansea–Rouen)	schooner	21.06.1824	50.32.05N 05.01.40W	Foundered	–	Rouen; coal; Capt. Poyd
Elizabeth and Jane	sail	10.10.1825	–	–	–	Penzance
London (Newport–London)	sail	09.06.1828	50.40N 05.00W	Foundered 'west of Tintagel'	Crew reached Padstow in ship's boat	Plymouth ; iron; Capt. Jobscott
Thomas and Jane (Cork–Southampton)	sloop	27.08.1829	50.37N 05.00W	Drove ashore, much of cargo saved	–	Cork; butter; Capt. Coleman
Pursuit	sail	05.01.1829	–	Lost at St Merryn	–	–
Catherine (Cardiff-?)	sloop	20.02.1833	50.28N 05.07W	Capsized in gale	Crew lost. Ship identified by bible found onshore	Cardiff; 80 Tns; coal; Capt. Daniel
Fly (Cork-?)	sloop	20.02.1833	50.28N 05.07.15W	Capsized in gale	–	Dartmouth; 40 Tns; butter, oats, hides
Mary Ann	sloop	20.02.1833	50.35N 05.00W	Foundered	–	St Ives; 75 Tns; Capt. Daniel
Agenoria (Sligo–London)	sail	10.10.1835	50.32.05N 05.01.40W	Drove ashore on Constantine Bay	All crew lost. Thomas Tummen drowned trying to get salvage	Belfast; 73 Tns; butter, oats (272 firkins saved); Capt. Fitzsimmons
Alert (Hayle–Shields)	brig	13.11.1840	50.27N 05.10W	Foundered	One survivor, a boy picked up by sloop	Sunderland; pyrites; Capt. Gregson
Unity (St Ives–Cardiff)	schooner	29.06.1843	50.35.02N 05.09W	Foundered	–	St Ives; 67 Tns; ballast; Capt. Thomas

Ship (route)	Type	Date	Position	Event	Crew	Details
Two Brothers (Falmouth–Port Talbot)	schooner	09.01.1844	50.35N 05.00W	Run down by a galliot	–	Brixham; 75Tns; Capt. Wheaton
Minerva (?–Wales)	brig	14.12.1844	50.28N 05.08W	Lost off St Eval	Crew of 6 lost	St Ives; copper ore; Capt. Quick
Manly (Plymouth–Newport)	brigantine	12.07.1845	50.32.05N 05.00W	Ran ashore in fog and went to pieces	Crew of 7 saved	140Tns; limestone; Capt. Sawyer
Ellie Marie (Newport–Indret)	lugger	05.10.1846	05.32.40N 05.01.40W	Hit rocks and sank on Harlyn beach		France; cast iron ingots/pigs; Capt. Joubert; Cargo auctioned on 28th inst.
Samaritan (Liverpool–Constantinople)	brig	22.10.1846	50.29.06N 05.01.55W	Struck Parkhead and was washed to Bedruthan Steps	Lost 8 of 10 crew	Liverpool; 249 Tns; textile cloth, copper sheet, tin plate; Capt. Davies
Spartan (Cardiff–Leghorn)	brigantine	23.10.1846	50.29.50N 05.02.46W	Ran on to Parkhead and broke up	Crew of 8 taken off by *Sir William Molesworth* of Padstow	Dartmouth; 142Tns; railway lines (half cargo recovered); Capt. Gellard
Brilliant (Hayle–Llanelli)	schooner	12.11.1846	50.35.00N 05.00W	Run down by an American barque	Crew lost	110Tns; copper ore; Capt. Jenkins
Amorous	sail	20.02.1848	–	Lost off Trevose Head	–	–
Sarah (Messina–London)	brig	18.01.1850	50.32.55N 05.02.10W	Ran ashore in dense fog on Constantine Bay	Crew stayed with the vessel and were saved	Newcastle-on-Tyne; 206Tns; lemons, lime juice, brimstone; Capt. Gibson
Emile Marie (Liverpool–Bordeaux)	chasse-marie	18.11.1850	50.49.51N 0504W	Broke up the west side of Trevose Head	Crew of 6 lost 4 inc Capt.	Sarzeau; coal; Capt. Carhoalent; Mistook Trevose for Lundy
Panja Eleusa	sail	22.10.1851	50.54N 04.59W	Foundered	–	–
Kitty (Charlestown–Liverpool)	Smack	11.11.1851	50 30 00N 05.05W	Collided with *Emma Jane* (Jersey) in F6 gale	Crew of 3 lost	Youghal; 44Tns; china clay; Capt. Strickland
Iris (Truro)	schooner	24.11.1852	50.40N 05.23W	Foundered 15m ESE Trevose Head	Crew taken off by *Honor* of Fowey	Truro; Capt. Stevens

Vessel	Type	Date	Position	Circumstances	Crew	Details
Malpas (Rouen–Swansea)	smack	10.02.1853	50.33N 05.02W	Collided with schooner Ono of St Ives. Sank	Crew of 3; one lost; survivors climbed aboard the Ono	Swansea; 48Tns; copper dross; Capt. Chalk; Loss £600, insured £300
Ariel (Cardiff–Elsfleth)	brig	30.04.1853	51.00N 05.07.45W	Blown up when fire damp ignited	2 of 3 crew were saved by schooner Auspicious	Elsfleth; coal; Capt. Warren
Regina (Neath–Plymouth)	schooner	20.12.1854	50.32.40N 05.00W	Drove onshore in F11 gale	6 crew saved	Plymouth; 90Tns; coal; Capt. Revely
Johanna	sail	11.01.1857	–	Lost on Mother Ivey's Bay	–	St Ives
Alpha	sail	11.01.1857	–	Lost off Trevose Head	–	–
Trader (Cardiff–London)	sail	18.9.1858	50.40N 05.01W	Abandoned 8m offshore	Crew saved in own boat	London; 117Tns; coal; Capt. Buck
Cherie (Cardiff–Rouen)	ketch	30.11.1858	50.32.45N 05.01W	Wrecked in Mother Ivey's Bay	–	Le Havre; coal; Capt. Gerrard
Mary (Swansea–Gibraltar)	brig	24.10.1859	50.33 00N 05.02.06W	Stranded and lost in F11 gale	Crew of 3 lost	Milford; 146Tns; coal
John Wesley	sail	26.10.1859	–	Lost off Trevose Head	–	St Ives
Iron Age (Newcastle on Tyne–Dublin)	brigantine	26.10.1859	50.35.00N 05.05W	Foundered	Crew of 11 lost	London; 339Tns; coal; (estimated loss £5,500)
Richard and Elizabeth	smack	26.10.1859	50.33.00N 05.02.06W	Sank in F9 gale 1m off Trevose Head	11 lost	Barnstaple; 19Tns; estimated loss £5,500
Unidentified	full rigger	26.10.1859	50.33 00N 05.02.06W	Sank near Cow & Calf	Crew of 16 lost	–
Alert (Cardiff–Gibraltar)	schooner	28.11.1859	50.47N 05.10.W	Abandoned 15m N of Trevose Head	Crew of 6 saved in own boat	Whitehaven; 123Tns; coal; Capt. Conning
Alice (Llanelli–Dieppe)	sail	30.11.1859	50.33N 05.02.06W	Foundered off Trevose Head	Crew saved by passing vessel & landed at Penzance	Folkestone; coal; Capt. Golder

Vessel (route)	Type	Date	Position	Event	Crew	Details
James Alexander (Liverpool–Calcutta)	full rigger	22.01.1860	50.30.16N 05.02.10W	After being disorientated in five days of gales, the vessel ran ashore at Porthcothan	One man lost of crew of 27	Liverpool; 1,089Tns; salt; Capt. Atcock
Pride (Porthcawl–Exeter)	schooner	02.06.1860	50.35N 05.00W	Sprang a leak and sank	Crew of 2 picked up by schooner *Aid* of Dundee	Exeter; 49Tns; Capt. White
True Blue (Teignmouth–Chester)	Schooner	07.07.1860	50.31.15N 05.12.40W	Foundered 7m W of Trevose Head	Crew saved in own boat	Teignmouth; zinc ore; Capt. Coysh
Caroline	schooner	15.01.1862	50.35N 05.00W	Sank after collision	Lost 5 of 6 man crew	101Tns; copper ore
Tartar (Falmouth–Liverpool)	schooner	10.03.1862	50.35N 05.05W	Foundered 4m off Trevose	Crew reached Padstow in own boat	86Tns; granite; Capt. Saunders
Gertrude (Newport–Southampton)	brig	1.11.1862	50.35N 05.00W	–	–	164Tns; coal; Capt. Snail
Eliza and Ann	schooner	15.02.1863	50.35N 05.00W	Foundered	–	Truro; 77Tns; Capt. Hocking
William and Ann	schooner	02.09.1863	50.34.30N 05.14W	Foundered	–	80Tns; iron ore; Capt. Jaco
Susan	dandy	28.11.1865	50.34.30N 05.14W	Stranded and lost in gale N F8	3 of 4 crew lost	46Tns; creosote
Volunteer (Swansea–Plymouth)	schooner	11.12.1865	50.35N 05.00W	Struck by SS *Minerva* and sank	5 of 7 crew lost. 2 survivors were only ones that could swim	Plymouth; 134Tns; coal; Capt. Skinner
Royal Albert (Calcutta–Liverpool)	full rigger	17.01.1866	50.32.40N 05.03.50W	Struck the Quies and sank	All 34 of crew lost	Liverpool; 1438Tns; tea, cloth, castor oil, shellac, India rubber, firearms; Capt. Davies; Insured for £160.000
Good Intent	sail	30.04.1866	–	Lost off Trevose Head	–	–
James and Mary	sail	2807.1866	–	Lost off Trevose Head	–	–

Ship (route)	Rig	Date	Position	Fate	Crew	Details
Mary Campbell (Liverpool–Aden)	sail	13.09.1867	51.04N 05.09W	Foundered	Crew of 20 and 7 passengers; Lost 7	Liverpool; 1,448Tns; coal
Active	schooner	07.10.1867	50.40N 05.17W	Foundered in gale F8	1 of 4 crew lost	60Tns; culm
Caroline (Newport–Salcombe)	schooner	11.10.1867	50.32.40N 05.03.30W	Struck the Quies on ebb tide	Crew saved in own boat	Padstow; 38Tns; coal; Capt. Watts
Sally	sail	23.01.1868	–	Lost off Trevose Head	–	–
Coronation (Porthcawl–Falmouth)	smack	15.05.1868	50.37N 05.00W	Sprung a leak and foundered	Crew saved in own boat	Bideford; 42Tns; coal; Capt. Cook
Electric Flash (Newhaven–Runcorn)	schooner	22.08.1868	50.44N 05.00W	Foundered in gale F9 10m NW of Padstow	Crew of 4 lost	Hayle; 60Tns; flints; Capt. Crenfel
Bretonne	sail	14.09.1868	–	–	–	–
Deitz (Cork–Cardiff)	barque	19.03.1869	50.35N 05.05W	Part of wreck was washed up in Trevose Bay	Lost crew of 12	Prussia; ballast; Capt. Grouen
Cornelia Maria	sail	16.05.1869	–	Lost off Trevose Head	–	–
Stephen and Elizabeth	sail	28.05.1869	–	Lost off Trevose Head	–	–
Victoria (?–Cadiz)	schooner	21.09.1869	50.31.05N 05.01.36W	Dismasted off Trevose Head and beached at Trevone	Crew saved by CG rocket brigade under Comm. Neate	Plymouth; 151Tns; coal 259Tns; Capt. Veal
Ann	sail	22.03.1870	–	Abandoned and sank off Trevose Head	Crew saved in own boat, landed Mother Ivey's Bay	Penzance; coal; Capt. Elles
Asterias (Cardiff–Hong Kong)	barque	21.05.1870	51.00N 05.10W	Burned out after gas explosion	Crew of 14 lost 2	800Tns; coal
Penguin	schooner	12.10.1870	50.35N 05.00W	Broke chains in M. Ivey's Bay and disappeared	Crew left boat at anchor	St Ives; 80Tns; Capt. Bryant
Superior (Neath–St Ives)	schooner	24.08.1871	50.35N 5.05W	Foundered in heavy sea 6m off Trevose Head	Crew of 4 rowed for 5hrs and landed at Padstow	St Ives; coal; Capt. Webber

Ship (route)	Type	Date	Position	Event	Crew	Details
Viking (Cardiff–Plymouth)	barque	02.04.1872	50.32.40N 05.00W	Ran ashore at Harlyn and broke up	Crew taken off by *Albert Edward* LB, lost one of 10 crew	Sunderland; 339Tns; coal; Capt. Gentle
Mary Ann (Newport–London)	schooner	16.01.1872	50.35N 05.05W	Sank after collision in F6 gale	Lost 1 of 7 crew	129Tns; railway track; Capt. Harris
Atlantic (Holyhead–?)	barque	01.04.1874	50.49N 05.20W	Foundered; identified by name board	Crew of 20 lost	Liverpool; 1079Tns; coal; Capt. Jones
Josephine (Cardiff–Newquay)	cutter	21.09.1874	50.34.18N 05.01W	Sank in gale 1.5m NE of Trevose Head	crew of 4 lost (all members of the Hockin family)	Padstow; 37Tns; coal 86Tns; Capt. Hockin
Creole (Neath– St Malo)	lugger	30.10.1874	50.34.45N; 05.01.30W	Sprang a leak, sank 2m NE of Trevose Head	Crew of 4 got off in own boat rowed to Padstow	St Malo; coal; Capt. Sene
Talbot	schooner	03.05.1875	50.35N 05.05W	Run down by unnamed steamer	Crew picked up by *Flying Cloud* of Jersey	Falmouth; 65Tns; Capt. Pascoe
Elodie (Cardiff–Barcelona)	barque	22.03.1876	50.35N 04.52W	Abandoned off Trevose, later washed up near Port Quinn	Crew of 11 got off in own boat landed at Padstow	Austria; coal; Capt. Seocolite/Socolich
Mary Ann; (Neath–Portreath)	–	19.03.1876	50.35N 05.00W	Leaked and sank	5 crew lost	St Ives; 91Tns; Capt. Richards
Paragon (Milford–Southampton)	smack	07.05.1876	50.36N 05.10W	Ship gutted by fire 6m NW by W of Trevose Head	Crew (2) in own boat were towed to Newquay by French lugger	Plymouth; charcoal
Thermuthis (Cardiff–Demarara)	brig	11.10.1876	50.32N 05.08W	Sprang a leak and was abandoned. Struck under Tregudda mine workings	Crew of 9 took to their own boat and landed in Trevone Bay	Brixham; 229Tns; coal; Capt. Corbines – later suspended by BOT inquiry for negligent abandonment
Alarm (Cork–Truro)	cutter	05.12.1876	50.28N 05.17W	Sank in F9 gale	–	Jersey; 30Tns; oars; Capt. Allen
Lizzie Male (Swansea–Fecamp)	schooner	29.01.1877	50.32N 05.08W	Dismasted 4m off Trevose Head. Later sank	Newquay LB *Pendock Neale* saved crew of 6	Padstow; 107Tns; coal; Capt. Male

Ship (route)	Type	Date	Position	Fate	Crew	Details
Pioneer	steam	29.01.1878	—	Dismasted and sinking 12m N of Padstow	Crew observed rowing lifeboat by schooner *New Parliament* but capsized and all drowned	Capt. Truscott
Marguerite Zelondide (Middlesbrough–Newport)	schooner	10.07.1878	50.47N 04.45W	Sank, leaking and overloaded, 18M NE of Trevose Head	Crew of 5 got off in own boat	Penzance; 98Tns; cast iron, pigs; Capt. Redman; (BOT inquiry said she was an old vessel, with a heavy cargo in a rough sea)
Leader (London–Swansea)	schooner	15.12.1878	50.32N 05.34W	Sank in collision with SS *Ben Medi*	Capt. and 3 crew jumped onto the deck of the *Ben Medi*. One of the crew, Peters of Devoran, drowned	Swansea; 108Tns; zinc ore; Capt. Bate; (BoT inquiry found the chief officer of the SS *Nat. Steele* negligent in navigation and suspended his certificate)
Hannah Louisa (Gloucester–Padstow)	trow	01.08.1879	50.35N 5.07W	Put ashore at Perranporth, later towed off by *Amazon* tug but broke line and foundered	Crew of 4 taken off by breeches buoy but went back on board with 4 others for the tow. 2 of the 8 men drowned	Chepstow; coal; 56Tns; Capt. Wheatstone
Maria (Porthcawl–Bordeaux)	sail	07.08.1880	50.32.42N 05.00.26W	Ran aground between Trevose and Padstow	Crew took to own boat picked up by *Pendock Neale* LB	Bordeaux; 92Tns; coal, coke; Capt. Lequimier
Rainbow (Llanelli–Shereness)	brig	29.09.1880	50.54N 05.22W	Abandoned in F9 gale sinking	Crew 6 fate unknown	Sunderland; 198Tns; coal 320Tns
Galatea (Swansea–CapeTown)	barque	05.12.1880	50.40N 05.12W	Sank after collision with SS *Edendale*	Crew of 12 picked up by the *Edendale*, ship's dog drowned	Swansea; 353Tns; Capt. James
Bessie Jane (Newport–Padstow)	ketch	18.10.1881	50.40N 05.01.50W	Lost in SE F10	Crew of 3 lost	Padstow; 41Tns; Capt. Phillips
Jackal (Preston–Natal)	steam	26.11.1881	50.35N 05.00W	Assumed foundered off Trevose	Crew of 10 lost	Glasgow; 181Tns; Capt. Downer FRGS; (maiden voyage of vessel)
Sainte Marie (Lorient–Newport)	ketch	21.01.1882	50.40N 05.10W	Sank after collision with SS *Durley*	Crew picked up by SS *Durley* and taken to Cardiff	Nantes; 129Tns; pit wood
Grace Darling (St Ives & ret)	lugger	29.04.1882	50.32.45N 05 01W	Anchored in Mother Ivey's Bay; broke chains and broke up	Crew of 7 taken off by Breeches Buoy	St Ives; 16Tns; Capt. Curnow; (Lifeboat was brought overland from Harlyn but not used)

Ship (route)	Type	Date	Position	Fate	Crew	Details
Zouave (Saundersfoot–Plymouth)	ketch	12.07.1882	50.47N 05.07.30W	Sprang a leak and sank	Crew of 4 abandoned vessel	68Tns; coal; Capt. Saunders
Japanese (Penarth Roads–Marseilles)	steam	2.11.1882	–	On fire near Trevose Head	Towed to Cardiff	London; coal
St George (Swansea–Nantes)	steam	28.11.1882	50.33N 05 20W	Foundered in F10 gale	7 of 17 crew got away in ships boat, 1 passenger lost	Glasgow; 548Tns; coal 525Tns, copper 100Tns; Capt. MacKean; (BOT inquiry found overloaded)
Brothers (St Ives & return)	sail	07.05.1884	51.00N 05.30W	Sank off Trevose Head	Crew of 6 lost (4 from same family)	St Ives; 11Tns; ballast; Capt. Trevorrow
Louisa	ketch	22.09.1884	50.49N 50.01.50W	Run down in dense fog by SS *Resolute* of Liverpool	All hands lost	Padstow
Mary Josephine (Penzance–Newport)	schooner	25.09.1884	–	Run down by SS *Ackworth* and sank	Crew plus Captain's wife rescued by SS *Ackworth*	Padstow; ballast; Pollard
Pearl (Poole–Bristol)	ketch	26.10.1884	50.32.30N 05.00W	Sank off Harlyn Bay	Crew saved in own boat	Plymouth; 44Tns; pipe clay; Capt. Roberts
Break of Day (Cardiff & return)	sail	15.05.1885	50.42N 04.56W	Sank after collision with SS *Ariel* in F7 gale	Crew of 3 fate unknown	–
Aeolus (Newport–Castellamare)	steam	05.08.1886	50.40N 05.03W	Sank after collision with SS *Valetta*	Crew 22 fate unknown	W.Hartlepool; 1,149Tns; coal; Capt. Malloney
Indus (Cardiff–Teneriffe)	steam	14.10.1886	50.40N 05.10W	Foundered off Trevose Head 9m NW	Crew 31 landed at Port Isaac by LB	Dundee; 2486Tns; coal; Capt. Leslie
Henry (Padstow & return)	pilot cutter	15.10.1886	50.35.50N 05.07W	Lost in SSW gale F9 while out seeking pilot work	Fate of 4 crew unknown	Bristol; 26Tns; ballast; Capt. Russell
Boswedden (Penzance–Wales)	schooner	16.10.1886	50.40N 05.01.50W	Foundered; Total loss	–	Penzance; 214Tns; coal; Capt. Dusting

Ship (route)	Type	Date	Position	Event	Crew	Cargo; Captain
Petrel (Leghorn–Leith)	schooner	09.12.1886	50.30.30N 05.02W	Broke up and went to pieces in Wine Cove	Crew of 7 lost 2	Belfast; 241Tns; marble (salvaged); Capt. Willis
Alliance	sail	09.12.1886	–	Sank off Trevose Head	–	Penzance
Leila (Newport–Newquay)	schooner	28.12.1886	50.44N 05.10W	Sank within 10 minutes of collision with SS *Alarity*	3 lost of crew of 4	Padstow; 70Tns; coal; Capt. Clemens
Valletta	sail	05.08.1887	–	Sank off Trevose head	–	–
City of Exeter (Penarth–St Nazaire)	steam	11.03.1888	50.37N 05.13W	Sank 8m off Trevose in W F10 gale	One crew saved by *Sarah Ann* a passing ship	Exeter; 1054Tns
Gleaner (Newquay–Padstow)	smack	14.03.1888	–	Went ashore on Towan Head	Crew of 3 plus passenger saved	Padstow; barley; Capt. Ivey
Grace Town (Penarth–Southampton)	sail barge	30.09.1888	50.40N 05.01.50W	Foundered 6 m off Trevose Head	Crew of 2 lost	50Tns; coal; Capt. Gallagher
Home Bay (Plymouth & return)	ketch	12.03.1890	50.40N 05.01.50W	Sank in collision with SS *Grantully*	Crew of 5 lost	Lowestoft; 73Tns; ballast; Capt. Dixon
Joseph and Marie (Hennebout–Newport)	brig	28.01.1891	50.44N 05.17W	Sank on collision with SS *Blairmont*	6 crew, fate unkown	France; 143Tns; pitwood; Capt. Allain
Fairy Belle (Cardiff–Par)	schooner	10.03.1891	05.26N 05.17W	Lost in the 'Great Blizzard' NE of Trevose Head	5 crew lost	Newquay; 90Tns; coal; Capt. Lewis
Crusader	brigantine	10.03.1891	–	Abandoned off Trevose Head in 'Great Blizzard'	5 crew plus Capt. picked up by *Gratitude* of Brixham after 19 hours in boat	Aberystwyth; Capt. William
Mary Sproat (Charlestown–Runcorn)	schooner	08.12.1891	50.30.34N 05.01.45W	Ran ashore in Treyarnon Bay	Crew of 5 lost 1; Manx sailor refused to jump for the rocks	Londonderry; 126Tns; china clay; Capt. Feeney
Countess Evelyne (Bilbao–Cardiff)	steam	13.05.1893	50.35N 05.05W	Collided with SS *City of Hamburg* in dense fog and sank	Crew of 18, lost 16; 8 passengers all lost, Capt. & first officer saved	Cardiff; 864Tns; iron ore; Capt. Evans
ES Lancaster (Newhaven–Cardiff)	steam	11.10.1894	50.32.40N 05.02.20W	Struck Trevose Head in fog and sank	Crew of 12 saved by ship's boat and LB	Cardiff; 294Tns; ballast; Capt. Kelley

Ship (route)	Type	Date	Position	Event	Crew	Cargo/details
Jessie McClew (Porthcawl–Hayle)	schooner	02.10.1895	50.32.20N 05.01,36	Drove ashore in Booby's Bay	–	Falmouth; coal 76Tns; Capt. Corbines
Sicilia (Liverpool–Barcelona)	steam	03.10.1895	50.30.36N 05.02W	Abandoned when cargo of slag coal shifted	Crew of 28 plus 1 passenger, picked up by *Arab* in two rescue trips	Liverpool; 2129Tns; coal; Capt. Silly
Unity (Cardiff and return)	sail	05.01.1896	50.40N 05.08.30W	Sank in collision with SS *Newlyn*	Crew of 3 lost	10Tns; Capt. James
Siracusa (Newport–Naples)	steam	03.03.1897	–	Foundered 'below Trevose Head' in heavy weather	Crew of 24 lost; Newquay LB forced back	Hamburg; 1,003 Tns; Coal; Capt. Rendey
Engineer (Fowey)	ketch	04.03.1897	50.28N 05.02.20W	Struck Park Head in gale	Crew 3 lost	Fowey; 39Tns; Capt. Toms
Ernest (Milford & return)	ketch, fishing	17.03.1897	(24m NW of T.H.)	Sank in collision with ketch *Thistle*	–	Brixham; 49Tns; arsenic; Capt. Tucker
Maria (Runcorn–Wadebridge)	Schooner	14.07.1897	50.35N 05.02W	Collided with the ketch *Ant*. Both ships sank	Both crews towed in to Padstow by tug *Red Rose*	Padstow; 81 Tns; coal + 3 passengers; Capt. Tabb
La Barrouere (Cardiff–St Nazaire)	steam	25.11.1897	50.44N 05.10W	Sank after collision with unknown vessel 10 m off Trevose Head	11 crew and a stowaway got off in a boat; Capt. and 4 crew picked up by SS *Thyrne*, en route to Algiers	Cardiff; 1,173Tns; coal; Capt. Young
Western Maid (London–Port Talbot)	schooner	25.11.1897	50.40N 05.10W	Almost certainly the vessel in collision with *La Barrouere*. Sank also	Crew of 6 picked up by SS *City of Liverpool*	Peel. IoM; 148Tns; cement; Capt. Doran
Westward (Waterford–Truro)	schooner	09.01.1898	50.52N 04.48W	Sank following collision with SS *Mandalay* of Whitby	Crew of 4	St Ives; 80Tns; oats; Capt. Nicholas
City of Bristol (Swansea–Rouen)	steam	24.09.1898	–	Foundered in gale	Empty long boat found off Park Head	Dublin; coal
Voorwarts (Cardiff–Genoa)	steam	03.01.1899	–	Abandoned off Trevose Head. Taken in tow by *Dragon*, broke tow & drifted to Bude	13 crew drowned, inc. Capt., 9 rescued by Newquay LB	Italy; 2,801Tns; Coal; Capt. Pittaluga

Rosshire (Cardiff–St Nazaire)	steam	04.01.1899	50.26N 05.10W	Sunk off Trevose Head in Collision with SS *Dugesculin*	One crew member crushed to death in collision	Glasgow; 2,080Tns; coal; Capt. Moxon
Dugesculin (Rouen–Swansea)	steam	04.01.1899	50.27N 05.10W	Sunk in collision with SS *Rosshire*	11 of crew of 23 lost	Rouen; 1,764Tns; ballast; Capt. Themoin
Monmouthshire	–	12.01.1899	–	Sunk off Trevose Hd	–	–
Bernard Barton (Chichester–Cardiff)	schooner	21.04.1899	50.42N 05.08W	Lost in SE F9 gale, 10 m NW of Trevose Head	Crew of 5 fate unknown	Bridgewater; 82Tns; wheat; Capt. Woods
Edith (Cork–Poole)	schooner	30.12.1899	50.47N 05.15W	Foundered in WNW F8 gale 18 m off Trevose	Crew of 3 saved in own boat	Chester; 60Tns; oats; Capt. Watkin
City of Vienna (Swansea–Rotterdam)	steam	08.11.1900	50.53N 05 00W	Collision with unidentified SS and sunk	Lost 18 of crew of 20	Dublin; 4,672Tns; sodium, coal; Capt. Cunningham
British Queen	–	19.11.1900	–	Sunk off Trevose Head	–	–
Whinfield (Decido–Cardiff)	steam	24.04.1901	50.32.45N 05.03.20W	Struck Quies in fog and sank	Crew picked up by Barry pilot boat and towed by tug *Active* to Padstow	Newcastle-upon-Tyne; 1,468Tns; iron ore; Capt. Gorvin
Norma (Newport–Fowey)	steam	28.01.1902	–	Foundered	Crew of 11 picked up by French collier *Racine* after 18 hours in ship's boat	518Tns; coal; Capt. Keast
Balhazan (Dunkirk–Cardiff)	steam	28.12.1902	–	Abandoned off Trevose Head	26 crew plus Capt. &wife rescued by *James Stevens No5* (Newquay) and *Edmund Harvey* (Padstow)	Liverpool; 2,096Tns; ballast; Capt. Maidstone
Pilot Cutter No.21	–	28.04.1908	–	Sunk off Trevose Head	–	–
Mistletoe (Milford and return)	ketch, fishing	14.09.1905	50.40N 05.15W	Sank in collision with unidentified SS 12 m off Trevose Head	4 crew fate unknown	Brixham; 47Tns; ballast; Capt. Lovell
Devonia (Brixham–Padstow)	ketch	10.05.1904	50.36N 05.10W	Sunk in collision with SS *Holmside*	Lost 2 of crew of 4; 2 brothers Dyer survived	Brixham; 41Tns; ballast; Capt. Dyer

Ship (route)	Type	Date	Position	Description	Crew fate	Cargo / details
AAD (Rotterdam–Briton Ferry)	sail barge	14.09.1895	50.35N 05.00W	On tow; sank in heavy weather	–	Neath; 150Tns; Capt. Ball
Belt (St Agnes–Chester River)	ketch	21.04.1906	50.32.42; 05.00.56	Struck pier on leaving port; was run ashore leaking 1 m E of Trevose Head	Crew of 5 saved	Beaumaris; 68Tns; nitrocake 120Tns; Capt. Foulkes
Shah (Cleveden–Littlehampton)	barge	11.09.1907	50.37N 05.04W	Foundered under tow	No crew on board	70Tns; ballast
Sam Weller (London–Briton Ferry)	brigantine	26.12.1907	50.43N 05.04W	Foundered after striking floating wreckage	Crew of 6 saved in own boat	Brixham; 141Tns; scrap iron; Capt. Loveridge
Europa	–	28.04.1902	–	Sunk off Trevose Head	–	–
Jilt (Glasgow–Teignmouth)	schooner	06.03.1908	50.50N 05.17W	Sank in collision with ketch *Condor* 20 m N by W of Trevose	Crew of 4 picked up by *Condor*	Douglas IoM; 79Tns; coal; Capt. Mylchreest
Martha	–	11.12.1908	–	–	–	–
Westward Ho (Padstow and Return)	sail	16.04.1909	50.42N 05.10W	Cut in half by Trawler SS *Picton* of Cardiff	3 crew lost of 5 inc. Capt. Morris; Frank Morris (son) and mate Lincoln survived	Lowestoft; 89Tns; ballast; (the wreck was hit by the ketch *Proceed* of Ramsgate)
Boucau (Bayonne–Barry)	steam	02.11.1909	50.50N 04.48W	Sank in collision with SS *Salyba*	Crew of 19 landed at Barry	La Rochelle; 1,151Tns; coal; Capt. Yeo
Venus (Garston–Frederickshaven)	barque	01.02.1911	23 m off Trevose	Sunk in collision with trawler SS *Triton*	9 crew fate unknown	Sweden; 327Tns; coke
Nathalie (Cardiff–Perros–Guierec)	ketch	15.12.1911	50.35N 05.05W	Sunk in collision with SS *Jessie*	Lost 3 of 4 crew	France; 59Tns; coal
Rostock	–	28.04.1911	–	–	–	–
Industry (Briton Ferry–Treport)	barquentine	27.09.1912	50.32.30N 05.00W	Stranded in Harlyn Bay and broken up	–	Swansea; 212Tns; coal; Capt. Erret

VESSELS LOST 1914–1918

Vessel Name and Voyage	Type of Vessel	Date Lost	Lat/Long	Location and Cause of Loss	Crew Saved and Lost	Miscellaneous: Registration, Tonnage, Cargo, Captain
Saint Marie (Swansea–Aiguillon-sur-mer)	ketch	27.05.1914	50.32N 5.07W	Abandoned off Trevose Head leaking; foundered	Capt., wife and 6 crew saved in own boat	Fecamp; 165 Tns; coal and fuel; Capt. Gilard
Perseverance (Port Talbot–St Nazaire)	brigantine	13.11.1914	50.48N 5.04W	Collided with SS Olkas and drifted to Trevose Head and sank	Crew of 5 picked up by SS Olkas	Erquy; 165 Tns; coal
First Prize (Falmouth–Runcorn)	schooner	18.03.1915	50.22N 05.18W	Foundered; total loss	5 crew saved, 1 lost	Plymouth; 227 Tns; china clay
Wiekawken	–	23.01.1915	–	Lost off Trevose Head	–	–
Francis	–	19.03.1915	–	Lost off Trevose Head	–	–
Vosges (Bordeaux–Liverpool)	steam	27.03.1915	50.42N 5.33W	Sunk by gunfire from U-28 23m W by N of Trevose Head	1 crew lost	Liverpool; 1,295 Tns; general cargo; Capt. Green
Drumcree (Barry–Port Arthur)	steam	18.05.1915	50.40.48N 04.59.50W	Sunk by two torpedoes 11m N by E of Trevose Head	Crew of 36 picked up by SS Ponto and taken to Cardiff	Liverpool; 4,052 Tns; ballast; Capt. Hodgson
Dumfries (Cardiff–Leghorn)	steam	19.05.1915	50.45.30N 05.01 35W	Torpedoed and sank 13m N of Trevose Head	Patrol boat HMS Kudos picked up 52 survivors, 2 lost	Newcastle upon Tyne; 4,121 Tns; coal; Capt. Kragn
Armenian (NewportNews–Avonmouth)	steam	28.06.1915	50.29.15N 05.33W	Sunk by gunfire from U-boat	Crew of 162, lost 29. Survivors picked up by trawler President Stevens	Liverpool; 8,825 Tns; 300 mules (for troops in France); Capt. Trickery
Magda (Port Talbot–Rouen)	steam	18.08.1915	50.39.30N 05.09W	Sunk by gunfire from U-27 8m N of Trevose Head	–	Tonsberg; 1,603 Tns; coal; Capt. Taraldsen

Name (route)	Type	Date	Position	Fate	Crew notes	Details
Sverresborg (Barry–Le Havre)	steam	18.08.1915	50.39.30N 05.09W	Torpedoed and sunk by *U-27* (*U-27* sunk by Q-ship next day)	—	Bergen; 1,144 Tns
Ministre Beernaert (Newport–Buenos Aires)	steam	26.12.1915	50.30N 05.33W	Torpedoed by *UB-24*	—	Antwerp; coal
Cottingham (Rouen–Swansea)	steam	26.12.1915	50.59N 04.54W	Sunk by gunfire from *U-24*	7 lost out of crew of 13. Patrol boat *Soar* picked up captain's boat with 6 crew	Glasgow; 513 Tns; ballast; Capt. Mitchell; (vessel was first to sink a U-boat by ramming)
Esmeralda (Par–Penarth)	schooner	29.04.1916	50.32N 05.21W	Sank 12m W by S in collision with trawler *Jane Ross*	Crew of 3 picked up by *Jane Ross*	Gloucester; 99 Tns; china clay
St Ansbert (Briton Ferry–Fecamp)	brigantine	30.11.1916	50.34N 05.33.30W	Scuttled by U-boat 20m W of Trevose Head	—	Fecamp; 275 Tns; coal
ELG	smack	1.12.1916	50.50N 05.30W	Scuttled by U-boat 25m NW of Trevose Head	—	25 Tns; ballast
T & AC	smack	1.12.1916	50.50N 05.30W	Scuttled by U-boat 20m NNW of Trevose Head	—	23 Tns; ballast
Euonymous	smack	30.01.1917	50.30N 05.31W	Sunk by gunfire from U-boat	—	59 Tns; ballast
Helena Samuel	smack	30.01.1917	50.30N 05.34W	Sunk by gunfire from U-boat 30m NNW of Trevose Head	—	59 Tns; ballast
Marcell C	fishing vessel	30.01.1917	50.45N 05.30W	Sunk by gunfire from U-boat	—	Ostend; 219 Tns; ballast
Merit	fishing vessel	30.01.1917	50.50N 04.36W	Sunk by gunfire from U-boat 20m NE of Trevose Head	—	39 Tns; ballast

Name	Type	Date	Position	Description	Casualties	Details
Trevone	smack	30.01.1917	50.50N 5.30W	Sunk by gunfire from U-boat 30m NW of Trevose Head	Crew of 2 lost	46Tns; ballast
WAH	smack	30.01.1917	50.50N 05.30W	Sunk by gunfire from U-boat 30m NW of Trevose Head	–	47Tns; Ballast
Wetherill	fishing vessel	30.01.1917	50.50N 05.30W	Sunk by gunfire from U-boat 25m NW of Trevose Head	–	46Tns; ballast
Ada	smack	01.02.1917	50.50N 05.30W	Sunk by gunfire	–	24Tns
Essonite (Caernarvon-Rochester)	steam	01.021917	50.38.45N 05.04W	Torpedoed by *U-55* 3m NNW of Trevose Head	Lost crew of 10	Glasgow; 598Tns
Inverlyon	smack	01.02.1917	50.47.30N 05.05W	Captured and scuttled by U-boat 15m N by W of Trevose Head	–	Lowestoft; 59Tns; ballast
Brissons	fishing vessel	12.02.1917	50.31.20N 05.16W	Captured and scuttled by U-boat	–	60Tns; ballast
Thrift	smack	11.03.1917	50.30N 05.16W	Sunk by gunfire from U-boat	–	40Tns; ballast
CAS	fishing vessel	12.03.1917	50.42.30N 05.05W	Captured and scuttled by U-boat 12m NNW off Trevose Head	–	60Tns; ballast
Ena	smack	12.031917	50.42.30N 05.05W	Scuttled by U-boat 10m N by W of Trevose Head	–	56Tns; ballast
Gracia	smack	12.03.1917	50.44N 05.07W	Scuttled by U-boat 12m NNW of Trevose Head	–	37Tns; ballast
Hyacynth	smack	12.03.1917	50.47N 05.10W	Scuttled by U-boat 15m NNW of Trevose Head	–	61Tns; ballast

Name	Type	Date	Position	Circumstances	Crew	Details
Inter Nos	smack	12.03.1917	50.44N 05.07.30W	Scuttled by U-boat 12m NNW of Trevose Head	–	59 Tns; ballast
Jessamine	smack	12.03.1917	50.46N 05.09W	Scuttled by U-boat 14m NNW of Trevose Head		61 Tns; ballast
Proverb	smack	12.03.1917	50.47N 05.35W	Scuttled by U-boat 25m NW of Trevose Head	–	24 Tns; ballast
Rivina	smack	12.03.1917	50.47N 05.10W	Scuttled by U-boat 15m NNW of Trevose Head	–	22 Tns; ballast
Lent Lily	smack	12.03.1917	50.45N 05.09W	Scuttled by U-boat	–	23 Tns; ballast
Nellie	smack	12.03 1917	50.45N 05.07W	Scuttled by U-boat	–	61 Tns; ballast
Elizabeth Eleanor	sail	13.03.1917	–	Sunk by gunfire 77 m NW by W of Trevose Head	–	169 Tns
Diligent (Santander–Troon)	steam	12.04.1917	50.43.30N 04.53W	Sank in collision with SS *Marquise de Lubersac*	Crew of 24, fate unknown	Sunderland; 2,184 Tns
Star of Freedom (Armed escort No 955)	sail – man-o'-war	19.04.1917	50.35N 05.25W	Struck a mine and sunk off Trevose Head	Crew of 10 lost	258 Tns
Plutus (Rouen–Barry Roads)	steam	24.04.1917	50.41N 05.07W	Torpedoed by *UC-47*; sank in 10 mins 9m NW of Trevose Head	Lost 1 of 17 crew picked up by patrol vessel, landed Penzance	1,189 Tns; ballast
Warnow (Penarth under sealed orders)	steam	02.05.1917	50.30N 05.10W	Torpedoed by *UC-48* 6m W of Trevose Head	Lost captain and 13 crew. 6 survivors were picked up after 2 hrs in water by SS *Duguesclin*	Dundee; 1,593 Tns; railway components
President	barque	06.05.1917	50.31N 05.21W	Sunk by unknown U-boat 12 m W of Trevose Head	–	St Malo; 354 Tns
Jeanne (Swansea–Nantes)	steam	09.08.1917	50.22N 05.20W	Sank in collision with SS *Echo*	21 crew; fate unknown	France; 576 Tns; coal

Ship (route)	Type	Date	Position	Cause	Casualties / survivors	Details
Wisbech (Cardiff-St Malo)	steam	14.08.1917	50.43.30N 04.53W	Torpedoed by *UC-51* 12m NE of Trevose Head	Lost 2 of 21 crew; Picked up by patrol vessel	Newcastle on Tyne; 1,282Tns; coal, patent fuel
Jane Williamson (Liverpool-Cherbourg)	brigantine	10.09.1917	50.32N 05.20W	Attacked by U-boat on surface 20 m NNE of St Ives	Crew abandoned vessel; U-boat fired on survivors killing 4 of 6 crew	197Tns; coal
Carl (Cardiff-London on tow)	German minelayer	07.10.1917	–	Ran aground at Booby's Bay after breaking tow	–	Hamburg; 1,933Tns
Poldown (Penarth-Boulogne)	steam	09.10.1917	50.31.35N 05.05.05W	Struck a mine and sank 2m WSW of Trevose Head	18 of 24 crew lost; survivors picked up by fishing boat and landed at Padstow	London; 1,370Tns; coal 1,700Tns; Capt. Watson
Altair (Rouen-Cardiff)	steam	18.10.1917	50.31N 05.17W	Torpedoed by *UC-64* 8m NE of Newquay	–	Kristiansaand; 1,674Tns; ballast
Pierre (Swansea-St Malo)	sail	29.11.1917	50.39N 05.04W	Sunk by U-boat at night	Crew landed at Padstow picked up by *Nellie Jane* trawler	Binic; 112Tns; coal; Capt. Piot
St Croix (Gothenburg-Passajes)	steam	12.12.1917	50.49N 04.49W	Torpedoed by *U-60* 13m NW of Trevose Head	–	Christiania; 2,530Tns; pulpwood
Ingrid II (Barry-Boucan)	steam	19.12.1917	50.35N 05.10.30W	Torpedoed by *U-60*		Kristiansaand; 1,145Tns; coal
Rewa (Malta-Cardiff)	steam (hospital ship)	04 01 1918	50.49N 05.10W (est)	Torpedoed by *U-55*	4 lives lost out of 207 crew	Glasgow; 7,267Tns; Capt. Drake
Townley (Devonport-Barry Roads)	steam	31.01.1918	50.48N 05.10.30W	Torpedoed by *U-46* (not seen) 18 m NE of Trevose Head	23 of 24 crew got away in ships LB. Picked up by *Ibis IV* trawler but 5 drowned while boarding her	Newcastle-on-Tyne; 2,476Tns; ballast
Cavallo (Swansea-Odda)	steam	01.02.1918	50.36N 05.10W	Torpedoed by *U-46* (unseen) 6m NW of Trevose Head	3 of 28 crew lost getting into boats; Boat with 7 picked up by *Holkar* smack; Boat with 18 picked up by Patrol Boat	Kingston upon Hull; 2,086Tns; coal, tin plate; Capt. Bradley

Ship (route)	Type	Date	Position	Fate	Crew/survivors	Details
Kindly Light (Honfleur–Milford)	sail	01.02.1918	50.38.30N 04.49W	Sunk by gunfire from U-boat 10m ENE of Trevose Head	–	116Tns
Holkar	ketch	06.02.1918	50.39N 05.10W	Sunk by gunfire from U-boat 8m off Trevose Head	Crew picked up and taken to Padstow	Lowestoft; 61 Tns; Capt. Tucker
Glenart Castle (Newport–Brest)	steam (hospital ship)	26.02.1918	51.03.30N 05.09W	Torpedoed by *UC-56*	94 of crew of 186 and 74 passengers of 94 lost	Southampton; 6,824Tns
Northfield (Glasgow–Devonport)	steam	03.03.1918	50.55N 04.45W	Torpedoed '25m SW of Lundy'	15 lost of 27 crew; survivors picked up by SS *Corvus*	London; 2,099Tns; coal 3,000Tns
Brise (Paimpol–Cardiff)	sail	07.03.1918	50.36.30N 05.03W	Scuttled by U-boat 3.5m N of Trevose Head	–	160Tns; iron ore, pitwood
St Georges (Granville–Paimpol)	sail	07.03.1918	50.35N 05.03W	Sunk by gunfire from U-boat 2m N of Trevose Head	–	Cardiff; 102Tns; iron ore
St Joseph (Fecamp–Swansea)	brigantine	07.03.1918	50.36N 05.08W	Scuttled by U-boat 5m NW of Trevose Head	Crew landed in Harlyn Bay	Fecamp; 434Tns; ballast; Capt. Guerault
Christina (Port Talbot–Bilbao)	steam	10.03.1918	50.22.20N 05.11.48W	Torpedoed by *U-55* 15m SW of Trevose Head	–	Bilbao; 2,083Tns; coal
Germaine (Swansea–Rouen)	steam	10.03.1918	50.36.50N 04.57.55W	Torpedoed by *U-110* 2m NW of Pentire	–	Caen; 1,428Tns; coal
Runswick (Newport–Barry Roads)	steam	18.04.1918	50.32.32N 05.03.18W	Torpedoed by *UB-109* (unseen); Broke tow and hit the Quies	Crew of 33 saved in own boats, later picked up and taken to Penzance	London; 3,060Tns; coal
Girdleness (Swansea–?)	steam	02.05.1918	50.45N 04.41W	Torpedoed 18m N by E of Trevose Head	Lost 2 crew of 35	Swansea; 3,018Tns; coal, patent fuel
Petersham (Bilbao–Glasgow)	steam	05.05.1918	50.25.05N 05.17.42W	Sank in collision with SS *Serra* 10m WSW of Trevose Head	Crew of 27 saved and landed at Padstow	London; 3,381Tns; scrap iron; Capt. Brewer

Rosendale (Par-Garston)	schooner	15.05.1918	50.38N 05.02W	Sank in collision with steam trawler *Cyrano* 5m N by E of Trevose Head	Crew of 6 picked up and landed at Penzance	Barrow in Furness; 150Tns; china clay
Tagona (Bilbao-Glasgow)	steam	16.05.1918	50.29.36N 05.04.38W	Torpedoed by *U-55* 5m WSW of Trevose Head	8 of 21 crew lost; survivors picked up by patrol boat and taken to Newquay	Montreal; 2,004Tns; iron ore
Mefford (Newport-Rouen)	steam	23.05.1918	50.28N 05.11W	Torpedoed by *UC-64* 7m WSW of Trevose Head	Captain and 7 crew landed at Newquay, rest at Mother Ivey's Bay	Skien (Norway); 720Tns; coal
Saphir (Barry-Bayonne)	steam	25.05.1918	50.34.27N 05.04.26W	Torpedoed by *U-94* 1.5m NNW of Trevose Head	–	Haugesund(Norway); 1,406Tns; coal; Capt. Holme
Brisk (Cardiff-Rouen)	steam	07.06.1918	50.45.51N 04.59.27W	Torpedoed by *UC-82* 13m NE of Trevose Head	–	Christiania; 1,662Tns; coal
Hunsgrove (Cardiff-France)	steam	08.06.1918	50.36N 05.11W	Torpedoed by *U-82* 6.5m NW of Trevose Head	3 lost of 40 crew; 34 arrived at Padstow and 3 at Penzance	London; 3,036Tns; coal; Capt. Kirkwood
Saima (Rouen-Barry)	steam	08.06.1918	50.29.05N 05.23W	Torpedoed by *U-82*, sank in 3 mins 10m W of Trevose Head	Lost 16 of 21 crew. 5 picked up by trawler landed at Penzance	London; 1,147Tns; ballast; Capt. Nelson
Orfordness (Rouen-Barry)	steam	20 07 1918	50.24N 0511W	Torpedoed 2.5m W by N of Newquay	2 lost of crew of 28	2,790Tns; ballast
Anna Sophie (Rouen-Barry)	steam	23.07.1918	50.31.42N 05.08.05W	Torpedoed by *U-55* 4m W of Trevose Head	Crew of 29 lost 1; Landed at Padstow in own boats	London; 2,577Tns; ballast; Capt. Martin
Portugal (Le Havre- Newport)	steam	02.08.1918	50.32N 05.07W	Torpedoed by *U-113* 4m WNW of Trevose Head	Crew 21 fate unknown	Antwerp; 1,463Tns; ballast; Capt. Godderis
Lake Edon (Barry under sealed orders)	steam	21.08.1918	50.27.33N 05.07.36W	Torpedoed by *U-107* 4m NW of Trevose Head	18 lost of crew of 35	USA; 2,371Tns; coal
Republique et Patrie (Swansea-Lorient)	ketch	24.08.1918	50.30N 05.06W	Collided with floating wreckage	Crew of 4 saved	Lorient; 40Tns; coal

Ship (route)	Type	Date	Position	Cause	Survivors / losses	Cargo details
Casara (Bilbao–Cardiff)	steam	25.08.1918	50.29N 05.07W	Torpedoed by *UB-92*	Lost 6 of crew of 26	Bilbao; 2,099Tns; mineral ore; Capt. Susaeta
Onega (Bordeaux–Swansea)	steam	30.08.1918	50.27.03N 05.14W	Torpedoed by U-boat 9.75m SW of Trevose Head	—	NewYork; 3,636Tns; pit props; Capt. Howard
Brava (Bordeaux–Cardiff)	steam	03.09.1918	50.34.35N 05.06.50W	Torpedoed by *UB-125* 4m NW of Trevose Head	44 survivors from *Brava* (20) and *Lake Owens* (24) were landed at Newquay in patrol boats	Lisbon; 3,184Tns; pit props; Capt. Rocha
Lake Owens (Nantes–Barry Roads)	steam	03.09.1918	50.34.30N 05.07W	Torpedoed by *UB-125* 3m NW by W of Trevose Head	Capt. Rocha and 30 crew landed at Padstow. Only 5 of *Lake Owens* crew were lost	Ecorse; 2,308Tns; ballast
Acadian (Bilbao–Ayr)	steam	16.09.1918	50.25.10N 05.15.58W	Torpedoed by *UB-117*, sank in 2 mins 11m W by W of Trevose Head	1 survivor of 25 crew picked up on following day by HMS *Wyre*	Montreal; 2,305Tns; iron ore; Capt. Green
Madryn (Penarth–Devonport)	steam	16.09.1918	50.38N 05.01W	Torpedoed by *U-82* 5m NNE of Trevose Head	Crew 25 got away in own boats landed at Bude and Swansea	Newport; 2,244Tns; coal; Capt. Harris
Lavernock (Bilbao–Glasgow)	steam	17.09.1918	50.28.30N 05.04.42W	Torpedoed by *UB-117* 5m SW of Trevose Head	2 survivors from crew of 28 picked up by SS *Wild Rose* and an armed trawler	Cardiff; 2,406Tns; iron ore
John O. Scott (Barry–Dover)	steam	18.09.1918	50.32N 05.16W	Torpedoed by *UB-117* 9m W by N of Trevose Head	1 survivor of 19 crew, after 9 hours in water picked up by motor launch	Newcastle-upon-Tyne; 1,235Tns; coal; Capt. Ross
Annie B. Smith (Swansea–St Brieux)	schooner	12.10.1918	50.51N 04.49.30W	Foundered	One crew saved out of 6	Ardrossan; 57Tns; coal

VESSELS LOST 1918 TO THE PRESENT

Vessel Name and Voyage	Type of Vessel	Date Lost	Lat/ Long	Location and Cause of Loss	Crew Saved and Lost	Miscellaneous: Registration, Tonnage, Cargo, Captain
Reine D'Arvor (Swansea–Fecamp)	schooner	28.10.1919	50.35N 4.53W	Lost both masts in gale 15m NW of Trevose Head; abandoned	Crew saved in own boat	Fecamp; 250Tns; coal
Emily	schooner	12.06.1919	50.35N 05.05W	Foundered	–	Padstow; 94Tns; Capt. Fitzpatrick
D P T (Lydney–Padstow)	ketch	26.06.1919	50.34.18N 04.59.44W	Struck King Philip Rock and then sank off Gulland	*Arab* stood by but crew got to Padstow in ship's boat	Bideford; 39Tns; coal; Capt. Screech
White Rose (Boulogne–Llanelli)	steam	20.03.1920	50.40N 05.00W	Sank after collision with SS *Fantee*		Liverpool; 2,691Tns; general cargo
Bratto (Penzance–Preston)	steam	25.11.1920	50.30N 05.07W	Abandoned leaking	Crew of 8 saved by SS *Woodburn*	Newcastle-on-Tyne; 202Tns; china clay; Capt. Hart
Voluntaire (Cardiff–Quimper)	schooner	09.03.1924	50.43N 05.12W	Sank after developing major leak	Crew of 4 got off in own boat, landed at Bedruthan Steps	Paimpol; 87Tns; coal
Smiling Thro' (Lowestoft fishing)	steam	20.04.1924	50.32.45N 04.58.50W	Drove ashore in dense fog. *Helen Peele* attempted to tow her off but was unsuccessful	Crew 9 got off in own boat	Lowestoft; ballast
Kalima	steam trawler	26.06.1924	50.35N 05.05W	Sank after striking submerged wreckage	–	Milford; 184Tns; Capt. Ball
Red Line No1	steam, oil tanker	23.01.1925	–	Capsized; turned turtle	one survivor C.O.Darragh picked up by *Theresa of Swansea*	Swansea; 300Tns
Cornish Coast	–	17.03.1926	–	–	–	–
Fageress	–	17.03.1926	–	–	–	–
Lord Devon	–	01.11.1926	–	–	–	–
Claretta (Cardiff–Granville)	steam	31.08.1930	50.32.30N 05.07W	Sank in collision with SS *Borderland* in fog 3m W of Trevose Head	Crew landed at Liverpool	Liverpool; 500Tns; coal

Ship (route)	Type	Date	Position N	Position W	Event	Crew fate	Origin; Tonnage; Cargo
Shoreham (Swansea–Rouen)	steam	31.08.1930	50.30N	05.15W	Sank in collision with SS *Annik* in dense fog 5m W of Trevose Head	Crew picked up by SS *Annik*	Liverpool; 805 Tns; coal
Sylvabelle (Trinite-sur-Mer–Cardiff)	schooner	01.01.1938	50.35N	05.05W	Abandoned after collision with SS *Ilse*	4 crew picked up by SS *Ilse*, 2 by MV *Cape Horn*. All saved	Bayonne; 125 Tns; pit props
Kai (Swansea–Southampton)	steam	01.02.1941	50.31N	05.07W	Struck submerged wreckage and foundered	Crew of 20; 10 picked up by St Ives LB; 8 by SS *Ilesman*. 2 lost	Gloucester; 1,251 Tns; coal
Empire Otter (Southampton–Avonmouth)	steam	16.02.1941	50.40N	04.51W	Struck a mine (probably British); sank 10m NE of Trevose Head	Fate of crew unknown	London; 4,670 Tns; crude oil
Tregor (Avonmouth–Hayle)	MV	04.05.1941	50.35N	05.10W	Abandoned after air attack; sank whilst on tow to Padstow	Crew of 6 fate unknown	Cardiff; 222 Tns; flour
Viva II	motorised yacht	08.05.1941	50.30N	05.22W	Sank following air attack	–	Requisitioned by Navy as Anti-Submarine Vessel
Svint (Workington–Plymouth)	steam	10.07.1941	50.38.26N	04.57.12W	–	Crew of 17 lost 1	Oslo; 1,174 Tns; coal and machinery
Risoy (Southampton–Swansea)	steam	20.03.1942	50.40N	05.01W	Foundered/torpedoed?	–	Mandal (Norway); 793 Tns; scrap iron 450 Tns
Liberator No.3	aircraft, US Navy	15.02 1944	50.35N	06.09W	Ditched plane	8 rescued, plus one body, by HSL 2641	–
HMS *Warwick*	destroyer (V/W Class)	20.02.1944	50.29.20N	05.25W	Torpedoed by *U-413* while on escort duty	Of the crew of 134, 67 were lost	UK; 900 Tns; Capt. Rayner
Ezra Weston (Avonmouth–Falmouth)	steam, US vessel	08.08.1944	50.40N	05.01.36W	Torpedoed by *U-667* in convoy EB6-66 and abandoned	Crew of 72 picked up by LCT except 4 officers who later landed at Padstow	New York; 7,191 Tns; 5,800 Tns army cargo and deck cargo of trucks; Capt. Larrabee
HMCS *Regina*	corvette (Flower Class)	08.08.1944	50.40N	05.01.36	Torpedoed by *U-667* as she stopped to assist the *Ezra Weston*	Of the crew of 85, 25 were lost	Canada; 925 Tns
Miles Martinet	target towing aircraft	08.03.1945	–	–	Ditched off Trevose Head	HSL 2641 picked up 2 survivors	–
Sturdee Rose (Garston–Plymouth)	steam	15.11.1945	50.35N	05.05W	Developed severe leak in heavy weather and sank	Survivors drifted for 8 days. 8 died in boat. Picked up by US *Tecumseh Park*	Liverpool; 877 Tns; coal; Capt. Alcorn

Name	Type	Date	Coordinates	Description	Crew/Rescue	Notes
Le Barbet	MV Fishing	02.04.1962	50.35N 05.05W	Foundered after developing a leak in a gale	–	Lorient; 355 Tns; ballast
HMS *Pheasant*	–	10.01.1963	–	–	–	–
Sheila	–	29.07.1963	–	–	–	–
Humbergate (Porthoustock–Bristol)	MV	02.10.1963	50.31.20N 05.13W	Cargo of stone shifted in heavy weather; boat listed and turned over 7mW of Trevose Head	Crew of 5 got away in life raft when LB was swamped	Kingston-upon-Hull; 200 Tns; granite chippings; Capt. O'Brien
Deo Gratias	–	24.11.1965	–	Capsized off Trevose in 70mph winds and 20ft waves	Povies and Bailey Trayes jumped to safety onto lifeboat	Trayes was to die later in the *Camelot Challenger* sinking off Stepper Point, 05.01.1992
Combesco	–	26.02.1966	–	–	–	–
Hemsley I (Liverpool–Antwerp)	steam	12.05.1969	50.31.24N 05.01.45W	Broke tow and ran aground	Crew climbed rocks to safety	London; 1,178 Tns; ballast; (Oldest SS on register being towed to breakers in Antwerp)
Northern Star (Hayle–Milford Haven)	steam	21.05.1969	50.31.24N 05.01.45W	Caught fire and abandoned	Crew of 2 taken off in Padstow lifeboat	Hayle; ballast
Lady Sylvia	MV, fishing	12.03.1991	50.34N 05.10W	Lost off Trevose Head on fishing trip; possibly swamped in heavy weather	Crew of 6 lost	Exmouth; ballast
Rose-in-June (Bideford & return)	MV, fishing	16.03.1992	51.00.13N 05.21.24W	Began taking water 32m W of Hartland Pt Assisted by *Charleen*, *Northern Explorer* and Padstow LB; sank	Crew of 3 taken off by Padstow LB	Fowey; ballast
Lia-G	MV, fishing	16.02.1993	50.29N 05.10W	Sank while hauling nets	Lost 1 of 3 crew, rescued by helicopter RNAS Culdrose	Weymouth; ballast; Capt. Semmens

Other titles published by The History Press

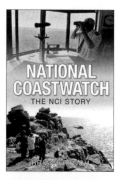

Coastwatch: The NCI Story
BRIAN FRENCH

The NCI is a voluntary body with a mission to reopen, develop and maintain a visual watch from th coastguard stations abandoned by HM Coastguard after extensive reorganisation in the 1970s. Followin the tragic and avoidable loss of two fishermen after a shipwreck at Bass Point in 1984, the NCI came int being and, in 1994, reopened Bass Point station. The NCI now boasts more members than the coastguar and operates closely with HMCG and the RNLI as part of the National Rescue Services. Split into tw parts, this book explains the history and development of the NCI, key figures, dates, incidents and th training and day to day work of the coastal agencies. It also shows the stations around the coast complet with maps and photographs.

978 0 7524 4929 6

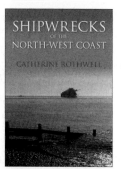

Shipwrecks of the North-West Coast
CATHERINE ROTHWELL

The north-west coast of England is renowned for its fierce storms with the inevitable loss of lif damage, shipwrecks, attending lifeboats and emerging heroism which such perilous situation aroused. Illustrated with photographs and images of ships, wrecks, mariners and ports and includin the recent high-profile wreck of the Riverdance, this book revises and expands work Catherin originally undertook almost thirty years ago, making it a unique guide to the shipwrecks of th north-west.

978 0 7524 5307 1

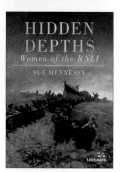

Hidden Depths: Women of the RNLI
SUE HENNESSY

For over 180 years images of strong, selfless males have populated the reports and literature of th lifeboat service. What has not been so well documented or recognised are the roles that women hav played in working to save lives at sea. The stereotypical image is of women waiting in the lifeboa house for their men to return – brewing tea and giving encouragement and solace to each other. Loo more deeply and it becomes clear that women have always been at the heart of the RNLI operatior undertaking a wide range of tasks which draw upon their distinctive skills and talents. From Victoria times right through to the twenty-first century, women have always been 'strong to save'.

978 0 7524 5443 6

Silent Warriors: Submarine Wrecks of the United Kingdom Volume Three
PAMELA ARMSTRONG AND RON YOUNG

The third in a comprehensive trilogy exploring the British Isles' submarine wrecks, this volum recounts the submarines lost along the coast of north Cornwall to the Isle of Man. Authoritative an meticulously sourced, wherever possible accounts are told in the words of those who were presen relating miraculous escapes from stricken submarines, relentless pursuit and merciless attack. We hea of the mysterious last patrol of UB 65, her fate as enigmatic as her spectral crewmen, as well as th last-minute escapes from UC 44 and H 47. Most poignantly of all, the book re-evaluates one o the darkest episodes of British maritime history, the loss of HMS Thetis in Liverpool Bay in Jun 1939 – revealing crucial new information on this disaster. An excellent reference guide for maritim historians and wreck divers, this series is an invaluable contribution to submarine history.

978 0 7524 5542 6

Visit our website and discover thousands of other History Press books.
www.thehistorypress.co.uk

The History Press